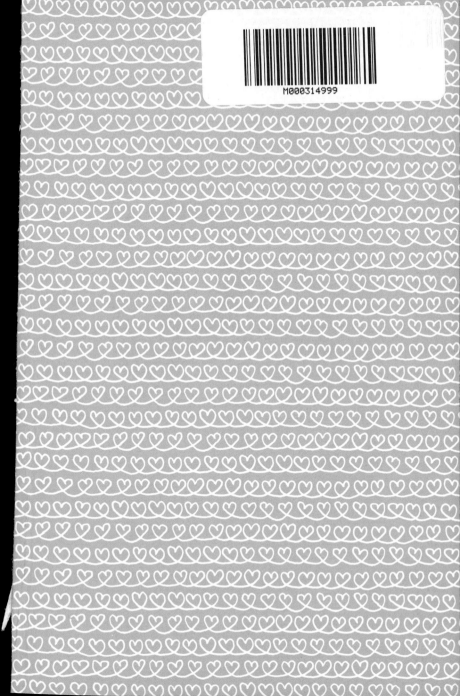

IF YOU FORGET EVERYTHING ELSE REMEMBER THIS

KATHARINE HILL

IF YOU FORGET EVERYTHING ELSE REMEMBER THIS

BUILDING A GREAT MARRIAGE

Muddy
Pearl

Published in 2018 by
Muddy Pearl, Edinburgh, Scotland.
www.muddypearl.com
books@muddypearl.com

British Library Cataloguing in Publication Data
A catalogue record for this book is available from the British Library
ISBN 978-1-910012-54-3

Typeset in Minion by Revo Creative Ltd, Carlisle, Cumbria
Printed in Great Britain by Bell & Bain Ltd, Glasgow

To Richard – #BFF

ACKNOWLEDGEMENTS

Writing a book is always a team effort and this book is no exception. Huge thanks to all those who have contributed in different ways, but especially to Rob Parsons for his wisdom and encouragement, to Paula Pridham, Robin Vincent, Rachel Harries, Samantha Callan and the incredible team at Care for the Family. And a special thank you to Sheron Rice, our Senior Editor, who brings her magic every time.

I am grateful to Stephanie and Richard Heald and to all at Muddy Pearl – it's great working with you. And thanks again to David McNeill for his wonderful illustrations which add such value and have become a feature of my books.

The book couldn't possibly have been written without the examples of many couples whose stories I have told – thank you to them. And many thanks to Richard, George and Ellie, Charlotte and Will, Ed and Catriona, and Henry who provide the real-life, real-time context for marriage and family life and make it so much fun!

'Give me a moment. I'm just checking whether there's anything in here about the perfect wedding night …'

CONTENTS

Acknowledgements VII

Contents IX

Foreword XI

Introduction XIII

Foundations, Foundations, Foundations 1

#BFF 5

Keep Connected 11

It's Good to Talk 15

Listening Says, 'You Matter' 21

Five Ways to Say, 'I Love You' 27

Speak Words of Life 31

Time Is of the Essence 35

Actions Speak Louder Than Words 39

Gifts – Not Just on Birthdays 43

Remember the Power of Touch 47

Vive la Différence! 51

Argue Well 57

Fight Fair 59

Find the Third Way 65

STOP – or Else! 71

Keep Short Accounts.. 77

A Slower Day Never Comes..................................... 87

Make a Date.. 91

Have Fun! 97

Lovers Not Flatmates 101

The Ten-Second Rule 113

The Price of the Affair... 117

Beware the Big Lie.. 121

Find Help on the Journey.. 127

Leave and Cleave 131

Look Back to Move Forward................................... 135

Discover the Money Secret..................................... 139

Know Where You're Going 145

Prepare for the Headwinds..................................... 149

When the Music Changes, so Does the Dance.... 157

Love Is a Choice 163

Appendix 169

FOREWORD

When Dianne and I were going out together, we dreamed about what it would be like to be married: we would finish work and return home every day to prepare a meal that would make the chef at the Ritz look better suited to working in a transport café. After dinner we would pull the chairs around the fire and discuss the hot issues of the day, go to visit friends or see the latest blockbuster. Finally, we would slip off to bed and begin another night of incredible passion. Our weekends would be relaxed and fun-filled.

The reality wasn't much like that. In fact, it wasn't remotely like that! We would certainly go to work every day, but we frequently got home late. And although our cooking was good (OK, *Dianne's* cooking was good), we'd regularly forget to defrost the meat or find there was nothing in the fridge so would end up having beans on toast yet again. As for the long conversations and the nights of passion … they were, to say the least, well spaced out.

I can't tell you how many couples are shell-shocked to discover that marriage isn't always the 'roses over the door' affair they imagined it to be. As wonderful as our partner is, we suddenly discover that they have flaws. We may even find that the qualities that originally attracted us to them now annoy us. When we first met them, we loved their carefree attitude to life; now we find them irresponsible at times. We once loved their strong character; now we find them stubborn! And in every marriage, it is inevitable that challenges will come along that can threaten our relationship if we don't handle them with care.

The truth is that we need to work at having a great marriage. I wish that Dianne and I had had a copy of *If You Forget Everything Else, Remember This … Building a Great Marriage* when we were first married. I'm sure it would be dog-eared by now. I love this book because in it Katharine does what she does best – she uses a solid foundation of research and expertise and applies it to the real world. Don't be misled by its apparently 'simple' style: it is full of good advice that deals with the really big issues that affect marriages.

Katharine brings to this subject not just depth of experience, but breadth and uses this to give us some key, easily-remembered principles. She makes us laugh not just at, but *with* ourselves, and with David McNeill's wonderful cartoons this makes for an incredibly enjoyable book. Dip into it often – it really will affect your marriage in a positive way.

Rob Parsons, OBE
FOUNDER AND CHAIRMAN OF CARE FOR THE FAMILY

INTRODUCTION

I was staying in a small attic room on the top floor of my parents' house. I woke up much too early with butterflies in my stomach. Saturday 27 April, the day that we'd been planning and preparing for so long had finally arrived. Through the gap in the curtains at the corner of the window I could see blue sky; our prayers for a sunny day had been answered – or so I thought. When I jumped out of bed and drew back the curtains, I realized that the patch of blue sky I'd glimpsed from the bed was the size of a postage stamp. Surrounded by menacing grey clouds, it heralded a typical British April day of sunshine and showers.

The rain held off until we reached the church, but during the service it poured. As my new husband and I knelt together at the front, the light reflected through the stained-glass windows, casting a rainbow over us and causing my mother-in-law to reach for the tissues one more time. And the variable weather continued throughout the day. Our reception was accompanied by bright sunshine alongside icy gusts of wind, and as we left for the Cotswolds in my much-loved blue Mini (decorated in shaving foam to within an inch of its life by my brothers), it began to snow.

Looking back over the thirty-three years since that day, it seems that the unpredictable meteorological highs and lows may have been a little warning to us of what lay ahead. Like any newly-wed couple, we were madly in love and imagined that this state of bliss would continue forever – our married life together would be one of continual sunshine with not a cloud in the sky. But, of course, for every couple daring to make those audacious wedding vows to each other, as well as times of glorious sunshine there will be periods of driving rain and snow. In these more difficult times, my husband, Richard, and I have been grateful for the wise advice of friends who have pointed us in the right direction. But we have also learnt many lessons the hard way, and in the early days of marriage I'd have loved to have had a book that I could dip into quickly – a compass to help us navigate the challenging adventure of married life. I don't suppose that either of us would have read a weighty tome on marriage, but we may have dipped into a short book that, like the ancient book of Proverbs, gave bite-sized principles for living – something that would help get us through the tough times and also make the most of our relationship. I very much hope that this is that book for you: a series of short chapters that bring clear and practical wisdom to every couple as we work at what is probably the most important relationship we have. So, whether you have been married for five minutes or fifty years, and whether you are currently basking in the sunshine or battling the storms, this book is for you. If you have a good marriage, I hope you will discover something to make it even better. I also hope and pray that there may even be something in this book that will turn around a marriage which is going through a difficult time right now. We have seen in Care for the Family that in a relationship that is spiralling downwards, it can sometimes just take one small thing to kick-start it in the opposite direction.

So grab a coffee, turn the page, and if you forget everything else about building a great marriage, remember *this* …

FOUNDATIONS, FOUNDATIONS, FOUNDATIONS

Ask anyone the first rule to follow when buying a house and they will tell you: 'Location, location, location.' In fact, in the popular television series of that name, the UK's choosiest home hunters, Kirstie Allsopp and Phil Spencer, spend considerable amounts of time searching for that particular quality: the right location for would-be homeowners.

But important as location is, something else is crucial. A house can have the best location in the universe – idyllic surroundings, breathtaking views and easy access to transport links and amenities – but if it doesn't have this next quality, the owners will be in trouble: it needs to have a solid foundation.

Foundations matter – and not just for houses. Construction workers will tell you that an important stage in building roads is when the foundations are laid. If they are substandard, the road will be unstable and fall in. Now, even if you've been crowned as your local pub quiz champion, I'd be surprised if you knew this incredible fact about the M6 toll road: according to the firm supplying the building materials during its construction, some 2.5 million Mills & Boon romantic novels were pulped and mixed into the tarmac to help with surface absorbency and ensure

'Foundations? Well, first do the dewatering, then sink the pylons. You'll need to pre-order your concrete well ahead of time ...'

a stable foundation that would withstand the heavy traffic.[1] So when you drive on this part of the M6, you are actually driving on a foundation of romance (well, of sorts, anyway!). Interesting as that fact may be, of much greater importance to us now are the foundations on which our marriages are built. A strong and secure marriage needs a foundation not just of romance, but … of love. The love we're talking about here isn't just the stuff of Mills & Boon. It's about a love that is robust. In fact, it's the kind of love described in a passage often read at weddings:

> *Love is patient, love is kind. It does not envy, it does not boast, it is not proud. It does not dishonour others, it is not self-seeking, it is not easily angered, it keeps no record of wrongs. Love does not delight in evil but rejoices with the truth. It always protects, always trusts, always hopes, always perseveres. Love never fails.*
>
> 1 CORINTHIANS 13:4–8

One characteristic of couples whose marriages have stood the test of time is that in many ways the success of their relationship has been of their own making.[2] They have been careful to deal with issues as they arise, and have been intentional in building on firm foundations. After all, it's not the wedding ceremony that makes a marriage, it's the people in it.[3]

Our marriages are all a work in progress, and in the following chapters, we'll explore what building on a foundation of love looks like in the real world.

---

1 'M6 Toll Built with Pulped Fiction', *BBC News online* (Last updated 18 December 2003). http://news.bbc.co.uk/1/hi/england/west_midlands/3330245.stm.

2 Robyn Parker, 'Why Marriages Last: A Discussion of the Literature', *Australian Institute of Family Studies, Research Paper No. 28* (July 2004).

3 Judith S. Wallerstein and Sandra Blakeslee, *The Good Marriage – How and Why Love Lasts* (Grand Central Publishing, reprint edition, 1996), p.330.

'Pleeeeeeaaaaase get me some chocolate.
I'll be your best friend!'

#BFF

The bus was late. I checked my watch one more time as I waited alongside a chattering group of young girls, all seemingly oblivious to the fact that they might be late for school. They clearly did not share my A-type personality. As the minutes ticked by, still with no sign of the No. 52, I watched them laughing together and catching up on the latest classroom romances. They were all dressed in regulation red sweatshirts and grey skirts, but that was where the similarity seemed to end. I couldn't help but notice how the fashionistas among the group were able to stamp their own style even on their school uniform. Whilst some were sporting sensible calf-length skirts, others had rolled up the waistband to create a hem that just skimmed the knicker-line. Some wore black tights, others were bare-legged and there was a mixture of footwear – wedges, heels, trainers and flats. Despite the range of attire, however, there was one thing that united this little band. It was the hashtag written on book bags, backpacks, wristbands and, in one case, on the back of a hand: #BFF – Best Friends Forever. This well-known abbreviation is often used digitally, but marketeers have also jumped on the bandwagon: you can buy #BFF bracelets, photo frames, key rings, mugs, coasters and more merchandise besides, all for the best friend in your life.

Whilst it's especially popular with teenage girls, #BFF is not a bad hashtag for a marriage. But the truth is that although it's relatively easy to have a #BFF at school, it's much harder to sustain that friendship over the length of a marriage. A friend remembers hearing Elsie Tanner, one of *Coronation Street's* most famous characters, point out to a young woman on the eve of her wedding: 'It's not just running around in a lacy nightie on the first night. It's all those breakfasts!' The truth is that couples who keep their love alive do so not by relying on the initial romance, important though that is, but by working on that #BFF thing.

A key factor in all of this is to continue connecting together and spending time in each other's company through activities we enjoy such as going to the cinema, a night in watching Netflix, playing sport, shopping, gardening, going out with friends or mealtimes together.[4] Richard and I first met when we started law college, and during the first year we found ourselves spending more and more time together. One of my favourite things to do on a Saturday would be to go out for coffee and, if possible, visit an art gallery. To my delight, I discovered Richard liked doing the same. We would spend hours in coffee shops and hunting out little exhibitions. It wasn't until after we were married that Richard confessed that not only did he not really like coffee (the difference between an espresso and a skinny latte escaped him), but he had no interest in art whatsoever (he didn't know his Renoir from his Rubens). But he'd wanted to please me and gave it his very best shot.

The same thing happened the other way round. As we got to know each other better, I discovered that Richard loved working with old cars – in fact, he started building a kit car. So I found I was spending weekends feigning interest in a Ford 1600 crossflow, overhead cam, twin Weber carburettor and other

4 Janet Reibstein, *The Best Kept Secret: How Love Can Last Forever* (Bloomsbury, 2007), p.129.

deep mysteries besides. I even began watching *Top Gear*! I hated the cold, the overalls and the smell of oil as I traipsed round freezing-cold scrapyards with him in the hunt for that elusive part he wanted for the dashboard, but it didn't seem to matter because I just wanted to be with him. As most of us do at the beginning of a relationship, we made the effort to be interested in each other's lives, and as we spent time together we became good friends – in fact, #BFF.

Relationship experts say that happy marriages are based on deep friendship.[5] Friendship is actually at the core of a strong marriage, and if there is a high-quality friendship in a marriage there is likely to be a high level of romantic and physical satisfaction. When we are friends, we look forward to spending time together, and when we genuinely like each other, we get more out of our life experiences because we have an emotional connection with the person who is sharing them.

Conventional wisdom says that having common interests keeps a marriage together, but whilst that's not a bad place to start, what really matters is whether that interest draws us together. It's not enough to just share interests with our partner; the key is how we relate to each other whilst pursuing those interests together.[6]

Whether couples have been married for six months or sixty years, it's often the little things that count – the small, everyday points of connection that bring them together and, over time, weave themselves into the very fabric of their marriage. Actress Simone Signoret described it like this: 'Chains do not hold a marriage together. It is thread, hundreds of tiny threads, which

---

5 Staci Lee Schnell, 'The importance of friendship in marriage', *Psych Central*, (Accessed 19 June 2018). https://psychcentral.com/blog/the-importance-of-friendship-in-marriage/.
6 John Gottman and Nan Silver, 'The Seven Principles for Making Marriage Work – Summary', *The Relationship Institute*, (1999). http://hametapel.com/gottman.htm.

'But we've been playing golf together for forty-five years.
I didn't know you hated it too!'

sew people together through the years. That is what makes a marriage last – more than passion or even sex.'[7]

Sharing in everyday moments builds our friendship and gives us a mutual history. My father died last year at the great age of one hundred, shortly after he and my mother celebrated their fifty-ninth wedding anniversary. He was a wonderful storyteller and never ceased telling his children, grandchildren (and anyone else who would listen!) the stories of how they met and the different things they had done together over the years. We all loved hearing them. Stories like this are characteristic of great marriages because they affirm the couple's happiness together and their friendship over time.[8] It's what anniversaries are for – not just a celebration of a couple's history, but also a joyful expectation of their life together in the future.

Walking hand in hand round art galleries and scrap yards, Richard and I felt so in love. I'm sure we thought it would always be like that, but like every couple, we hit some difficult patches. During those times, it has helped us to be able to look back and remember the stories and experiences we've shared, and the friendship that brought us together in the first place.

In the ups and downs of married life, it's a good principle to remind ourselves that we are friends. It's not just because we laugh together, sometimes hurt each other, have fun together and share interests. It's because, at the end of the day, we know that when trouble comes there is someone who has got our back, someone who is there for us come what may – in short, our #BFF.

7 Simone Signoret talking to David Lewin, *The Daily Mail*, 4 July 1978, p7.
8 Wallerstein and Blakeslee, *The Good Marriage – How and Why Love Lasts*, p.324.

'OK, I love you too, but can I call you back in a while,
I'm kind of in the middle of a thing ...'

KEEP CONNECTED

Banksy, the famous undercover Bristol graffiti artist, painted an iconic picture on a wall outside a boys' club in Bristol. *Mobile Lovers* is a picture of a couple embracing and checking their mobile phones over each other's shoulder at the same time. With the acerbic wit and skill that made him famous, Banksy was highlighting an issue that can drive a coach and horses through every marriage. It is the issue of communication.

'Communication' is very much a buzzword, but it comes from the Latin verb *communicare* – to share. At Care for the Family, we receive heartbreaking emails or phone calls every day from those facing difficulty in their family life, particularly in their marriages. Often there's a bigger picture, but time and again when they look back, people say that the problems began with a lack of communication – an inability to share.

One woman, Lesley, wrote:

The first couple of years of our marriage were everything we hoped they'd be. We set up home and both had jobs we enjoyed. Then Sam was born and I stayed at home to look after him. Lee was promoted and had to work longer hours. I made a life for Sam and myself at home. Lee and I didn't have much time together, and I can see now that we began to live separate lives. It's as if we don't know each other any more. We've stopped communicating about things that matter.

Sadly, Lesley's story is not unusual. Lack of communication can make two people who once loved each other deeply feel like complete strangers. When one finally looks up and reaches out to the other, they can find that the love between them has died. Good communication, on the other hand, is at the heart of a healthy relationship. If we learn to keep communicating well, we are likely to feel connected to each other and, individually, we'll feel more secure, confident and cared for.

We often make the very reasonable excuse that 'life is just so busy', yet I have discovered that couples whose marriages thrive *make* time to communicate. An extreme example (but one of my favourites!) is the relationship of Prime Minister Winston Churchill and his wife Clementine. Their fifty-six-year marriage thrived despite the difficulties of British politics and the challenge of leading the country through the Second World War, and this was due, at least in part, to their keeping in constant communication when they were away from each other. It was before the days of the smartphone, so texting or FaceTime calls were not an option, but Winston and Clementine kept in touch through the art and discipline of letter-writing. These affectionate letters (many of which can be read today) give insights into the depth and intimacy of their relationship. Most end with ink drawings illustrating their pet names for each other. He was her 'pug' and she was his 'cat'.

Winston wrote this letter to Clementine on 23 January 1935 when she was travelling abroad:

My darling Clemmie, in your letter from Madras you wrote some words vy dear to me, about my having enriched yr life. I cannot tell you what pleasure this gave me, because I always feel so overwhelmingly in yr debt, if there can be

accounts in love … What it has been to me to live all these
years in yr heart & companionship no phrases can convey.[9]

With their busy schedules and weighty responsibilities, I don't imagine it was easy to find time to write, but find time they did. They made a habit of sharing with each other all that they were doing, thinking and feeling. Good communication was the bedrock of their marriage.

We live in a digital age and the use of technology has woven itself into our most intimate relationships. It can present us with huge challenges but also many opportunities. My role at Care for the Family means that I am often away on the road speaking at our events, so Richard and I have to try and carefully navigate our relationship through those times. We now have a PhD in the art of miscommunication and misunderstanding caused by being apart. We don't always get it right, but what we've learnt is that communicating every day, and by any means possible (phone calls, texting, WhatsApp, Skype), fuels our marriage and keeps us in step. With conflicting work schedules, trying to keep this up is not for the faint-hearted. Richard is generally at work all day, and the time when he gets home usually coincides with the need for me to do a sound check and begin the evening event. We have discovered that we have to be intentional and disciplined about staying in contact, otherwise we drift apart and are irritable with each other when we're back together at the weekend. It will look different for every couple, but we've worked out through trial and error that the best way for us to stay connected when I'm on the road is to try to speak first thing in the morning – before breakfast for me and when Richard is on his way to work.

9 Mary Soames, *Clementine Churchill – The Revised and Updated Biography* (Random House, 2011), p.292.

Perhaps we would all do well to take advice from broadcaster Libby Purves: 'The only real essential [in marriage] is to carry on the conversation you started.'[10]

But how do we carry on that conversation? In other words, what does good communication looks like? Three key features are:

1. Listening well – i.e., paying attention and 'getting' what the other person is trying to say.

2. Keeping each other up to date with the everyday bits and pieces of information that affect how you do life together.

3. Telling each other your deepest and most significant thoughts and feelings.[11]

We'll take a closer look at two important aspects of good communication, talking and listening, in the next two chapters.

---

10 Libby Purves, *Nature's Masterpiece: A Family Survival Book* (Hodder, 2000), p. 221–2.
11 Janet Reibstein, *The Best Kept Secret: How Love Can Last Forever*, p.98.

IT'S GOOD TO TALK

Oscar Wilde said: 'Ultimately, the bond of all companionship, whether in marriage or friendship, is conversation.'[12] Just how important conversation is in a happy relationship came home to me very clearly when I was working as a family lawyer; every day I would meet people who felt their marriage was at an end. I will always remember a morning in November when a man came into my office. I asked him how I could help and without uttering a word he reached into his pocket, pulled out a brown envelope, and pushed it across the desk towards me. Inside was a crumpled piece of paper; it looked as if it had been read time and again. It was a letter from his wife:

> *I'm sorry it's had to end like this, but I can't carry on. We've both changed, and I don't think I know who I am any more. I've tried to talk with you, but you haven't wanted to listen. It's as if we don't know each other any more. We've stopped talking about things that matter.*

I imagine that when they were first married this couple would have spent hours just talking, but over time they had somehow 'lost' each other. There had come a point when they either couldn't, or wouldn't, talk.

12 Oscar Wilde, et al, *The Complete Works of Oscar Wilde: De profundis, 'Epistola: in carcere et vinculis'* (Oxford University Press, 2000), p.46.

So many people, especially women, have spoken or written to us at Care for the Family about this issue. I can summarize what they say in a few sentences because the words are often so similar: 'I'm lonely. I've been in this marriage for ten/twenty/ thirty years. We've made a home together; we've made love together; we've had children together. And yet I'm lonely – we just don't talk any more.'

Dr Philip Zimbardo, Professor of Psychology at Stanford University, said: 'I know of no more potent killer than isolation. There is no more destructive influence on physical and mental health than the isolation of you from me.'[13] We become isolated when we become so self-absorbed and closed-in on ourselves that we are unable to share in any meaningful way with our husband or wife. And isolation is shatteringly powerful in its impact: it destroys not only the person who has withdrawn into themselves, but also the person who feels excluded.

One woman said of her husband:

He has made me into an island. He will not talk to me about anything. In the early years of our marriage, we would spend hours talking together, but something has happened to him. It seems he can't talk to me … Have you any idea what it is like to share your home, your body, your life with somebody who will not communicate with you? Eventually you die inside.[14]

Richard and I went for a cup of coffee in our local Starbucks recently. After reading and deciphering the extensive coffee menu, we opted for a skinny flat white and a full fat cappuccino

13 Dr P. Zimbardo, 'The Age of Indifference', *Psychology Today* (August 1980), p.71–76.
14 Rob Parsons, *The Sixty Minute Marriage* (Hodder & Stoughton, 2009), p.21.

(no chocolate). Richard stayed at the counter to collect our order, and I grabbed the only free table. As I looked around the cafe, I realized every other table was occupied by couples, all of whom were sitting opposite each other in silence, engrossed in the screens of their mobile phones. Maybe some were dealing with important work emails – we'd done the same thing on many occasions. But as I reflected on the scene, I was pretty sure that if my fellow customers had been having coffee with someone they didn't know so well, they would have put their phones on silent and made the effort to talk. It's interesting because the person we should make the most effort to talk to is, of course, our partner. As Richard came over with the coffee, I felt my phone buzz in my pocket. Automatically, my hand reached to answer it; I was desperate to see who it was who needed my immediate attention, but then I thought, 'No,' as I realized something: the person I needed to focus on was sitting right in front of me.

Real communication in marriage means talking to each other about all parts of our lives – sometimes even the parts we would rather keep hidden. Our individual personalities – whether we are extroverts or introverts, logical or intuitive – will have an impact on our style of communication and make it easier for some of us than others. We will also be affected by the way communication was modelled to us in the homes we grew up in.

Marianne reflects:

I am an introvert and I grew up in a home where feelings weren't really expressed. In the early years of marriage, I found I didn't really know how to talk to my husband, Dave. I didn't even have a vocabulary for identifying my feelings. I didn't share my private thought-life with anyone, not even with him. Gradually this began to create a distance between us. However, over the years I've come to realize the difference that talking about things openly can make to our marriage. It's not been easy, but little by little, and with a lot of practice and encouragement from Dave, I have learnt to let down my guard and to talk – not just about everyday things but about how I feel, about deeper stuff. I have learnt to share my hopes and dreams and even some of my fears. Voicing these things has brought us to a place of connection in our marriage that I previously wouldn't have thought possible.

Of the two of us, it is probably Richard who finds it more difficult to talk about how he feels; *my* challenge is listening. When Richard comes home from work, I will usually ask him how his day has been and for the last thirty-plus years his reply has been the same: 'Fine.' In his defence, it may well have been fine, and rather than carrying out an autopsy of the day, he needs to unwind by putting on his jeans, turning on the TV or rummaging in the fridge for something to keep hunger at bay. My default position after a day at work is generally the polar opposite. With the key still in the door and my coat still on, I will download the entire day – what the journey to work was like; what meetings I had and how they went; how much I liked a colleague's new jacket; news of an engagement announcement; how quickly I managed to do the crossword at lunchtime; the contents of a difficult email exchange and how it made me feel; and, finally, a résumé of the traffic on the journey home – all without drawing breath.

For some of us, learning to talk about how we feel may not be an issue, but for others it can take courage to make ourselves vulnerable. When our children were growing up, they would

'Don't you dare say your day was "fine."'

often tell me that my most annoying habit was asking too many questions. Interrogations about what they did at school or on a Saturday night in town would rival cross-examination by a QC at the Old Bailey. But although it might be an irritation to teenagers who are trying to spread their wings, the ability to ask questions can be a decided advantage in a marriage.

We need to be interested in our spouse and in their day – even if the aerodynamics of the prototype they are working on, staff room politics or the long line at Asda aren't top of the list of things we'd naturally find interesting. Timing (mealtimes are often good) and sensitivity are all important, but we can gradually draw our partner out by allowing them to share and express how they feel – perhaps by asking how a meeting went or how they got on with their new colleague. It takes effort and it takes practice, but it's the way to build connection in a marriage.

It's good to talk!

LISTENING SAYS, 'YOU MATTER'

The philosopher Paul Tillich said: 'The first duty of love is to listen.' Listening is vital to good communication.

We went to a friend's birthday party recently. We'd been thrilled to be invited but were also pleased because it would give us the chance to catch up with an old acquaintance we hadn't seen for years. I set off on a quest to seek her out and when I found her we began talking, but after a few minutes I realized that her attention had wandered. I thought for a moment that she was admiring my scarf (a purchase I'd been rather pleased with!), but then realized my mistake – she was looking at a group of people just behind me. I battled on talking to her for a few minutes and then gave up the unequal struggle, stepping aside to let her join in with what I assume she thought was a much more interesting conversation. Whilst her distraction and failure to listen was disappointing, my main feeling was an overwhelming sense of insignificance and unimportance.

This was in sharp contrast to the conversation I had an hour or so later at the table. I was sitting next to James, a photographer. We had mutual friends but had never had a one-to-one conversation. He was both interesting and *interested*. He asked good questions and listened carefully to my replies. He has been described as a 'there you are' not a 'here I am' person.

There is a story of a woman who dined on different occasions with the political rivals William Ewart Gladstone and Benjamin Disraeli. When she was asked to give her impressions of the men, she replied, 'When I left the dining room after sitting next to Gladstone, I thought he was the cleverest man in England. But after sitting next to Disraeli, I thought I was the cleverest woman.' Being listened to gives us an incredible feeling of worth and value. And that means that every day, just by listening to our husband or wife, we have at our disposal the power to make them feel loved and valued.

But if we are to listen well, there are some practical tips we can learn that will be of help. Richard and I were having a meal with a wonderful couple, Margaret and Roger, when the topic of conversation turned to marriage. They had recently celebrated their golden wedding, and we asked them if they would share any lessons they had learnt. They told us about various little acts of kindness and big acts of forgiveness, but one story in particular caught my attention. Margaret explained that she had been a teacher when they were first married. Anxious to impress the headmaster and do her best for her class, she would ask Roger to listen to her whilst she gave an overview of her lessons for the following day. He would sit at the kitchen table with a cup of tea and the newspaper in front of him, and she would begin. After a few moments, his eyes would invariably wander to the headlines, and if he thought she wasn't looking, a quick flick of the wrist would take him to the sports page. 'He believed he was listening,' Margaret said, 'But he wasn't. I needed him to listen with his eyes.' Looking at Margaret and Roger now, with fifty years of marriage behind them, I realized that lesson had been one they had learnt and never forgotten. As she spoke, his eyes didn't flinch from hers. What she said

'Hang on. Is this one of those "I don't want
you to solve my problem" conversations?'

has stayed with me over the years and I've tried to put listening with my eyes into practice with my children, with friends, with colleagues and with Richard.

If giving eye contact is a good habit to learn, there are also a few bad habits to avoid and we'll look at three of them now.

1. Interrupting

In the book of Proverbs it says: 'To answer before listening – that is folly.'[15] The writer obviously knew something about human nature since the average person apparently listens for just seventeen seconds before interrupting.[16] I think my average is nearer five! If Richard is talking, instead of really listening, I so easily find myself marshalling my thoughts on how to respond, thinking of a good story that illustrates what he's saying, working out what to say next, and then launching in with my views rather than waiting for him to finish. This certainly doesn't give him the feeling that he's being listened to.

2. Fixing the problem

I am an 'external processor', which means that I talk through my thinking process when I'm working out a problem. A while ago, I had to make a difficult decision about a family situation. I'd go home in the evening and rehearse all the options with Richard, then he would interject with what he saw as excellent, wise and timely advice. To his dismay, although he thought the problem had been dealt with the night before, the same thing would happen the next day – I'd come home and start talking through all the different options. What he failed to understand was that on occasions like this, I don't usually need the problem

15 Proverbs 18:13.
16 Nicky and Sila Lee, *The Marriage Book* (Alpha International, 2009), p.62.

to be fixed, however excellent the advice. I can often work out the solution myself. What I *do* need is someone who will simply … listen.

3. Making assumptions

A University of Chicago study discovered that complacency can be a problem among married couples.[17] We assume we are on the same page, so we either don't bother to properly explain what we mean or don't bother to really listen. Added to that, we each have our own opinions which can act as a filter, stopping us listening to what our partner is actually saying and the feelings behind it. A good way to really pay attention to them is to reflect what they are saying back to them: 'So, what I'm hearing is that …' or 'It sounds like you …'

There will be plenty of people in the world who want us to listen to them, but far fewer who will listen to *us*. One of the greatest gifts we can give to our husband or wife is to be that person in their lives who they can rely on to ask how they are … and then wait to hear the answer.

17 'What You Can Learn from Marriage Studies', *Woman's Day* (18 February 2011). https://www.womansday. com/relationships/dating-marriage/advice/a5528/what-you-can-learn-from-marriage-studies-116044/.

'Aaah, coffee. The sixth love language.'

FIVE WAYS TO SAY, 'I LOVE YOU'

At Care for the Family we have spoken to tens of thousands of couples over the years regarding a concept written about by psychologist Gary Chapman in his book *The 5 Love Languages*.[18] Chapman's theory is that we all have different ways of giving and receiving love. It is a simple but profound idea with the potential to transform our relationships.

When Chapman asked couples in his counselling practice how they wanted their husband or wife to show them love, he noticed that their answers fell into five categories which he called the five 'love languages':

1. Words of affirmation: words of thanks, praise or appreciation.

2. Quality time: just being with our partner and spending time together.

3. Acts of service: practical or helpful tasks that show that we care.

---

18 Gary Chapman, *The 5 Love Languages: The Secret to Love that Lasts* (Moody Press, 2015).

4. Gifts: they don't have to be expensive – it is the thought behind the gift that counts.

5. Physical touch: physical contact – a brush on the shoulder, holding hands, a hug, sex.

In the same way that we speak a first language, each of us has a primary *love* language; one or two of these five categories will be the way we most naturally communicate and understand love. But there is a problem. In our marriages, we often try to show our husband or wife that we love them by using *our* love language – the way *we* feel loved. We assume our way of showing love is the same as theirs, and then we feel frustrated when they don't seem to appreciate our efforts. It can be as if we are speaking in a foreign language to them; we are speaking English when they only speak Japanese. They will never understand.

For Richard and I, understanding this concept was a light bulb moment in our marriage. We realized for the first time that we had different ways of feeling loved so, despite our best intentions, we had not been communicating love in a way that we each understood. Whilst my primary ways of feeling loved are through words and gifts, Richard's were actions and touch. Messages of undying love I had written on beautiful handmade paper were water off a duck's back to him, and I wouldn't even notice when he had tidied the kitchen or cut the grass in an effort to demonstrate his love for me. Affirming words don't communicate love to him; thoughtful actions don't do it for me.

Like us, many – perhaps most – partners find they have different ways of giving and receiving love, but the solution is simple: we need to learn the other's language. We can study our husband or wife a little – discover the way they best receive love

– and then act on that. Of course, just like learning a foreign language, expressing love in a new way can be hard work at first. It might feel awkward and take practice, but it will be worth it to have a marriage where we both feel loved.

We'll look at the five ways to say I love you in the next few chapters.

'"You missed a bit" is not encouraging!'

SPEAK WORDS OF LIFE

It was Mark Twain who reportedly said: 'I can live for two months on a good compliment.' Positive and affirming words can communicate love powerfully for some people. Another of the ancient proverbs says, 'Our words have the power of life'[19] and if words are important to us, praise or encouragement from our husband or wife will have a positive impact on our marriage – perhaps more than we could ever imagine.

Rob Parsons, the founder and chairman of Care for the Family, tells the story of a trip into the Sinai Desert. The guide showed him an amazing plant which has learnt how to survive with very little water. It does this by 'dying' in sections. If no rain comes, half of the plant will close down and the rest is then able to use whatever moisture it can find. As the drought continues, other parts of the plant shut down too until finally there might be just a single stem left. But when the rains come – when a single drop of water hits it – the seedpods on that stem explode with new life.

There may be a drought in some of our marriages – a drought of positive words. And like the plant, parts of the marriage begin to shut down and die. But choosing to make the effort to speak kind, encouraging and positive words to our husband or wife – especially if their love language is words – can bring new life to a marriage.

19 Proverbs 18:21 (author's paraphrase).

If words of affirmation aren't our primary love language, and particularly if we have grown up in a home where there has been little encouragement or praise, we may need to practise and be intentional about speaking positive words to our partner, but it will be worth it.

One of the things I love about Richard is that he's quick with his words – he can usually be relied upon to be the life and soul of the party. And he often says kind and encouraging things to and about me – life-giving things – which make me feel loved. But not always …

It was my birthday and we agreed to go out for a meal with some friends to celebrate. We met them at the restaurant and they handed me a card and a present. Inside the card they had written a long list of wonderful things about me. I have to admit that it was completely over the top, but it made me feel a million dollars – loved, valued and special. I thanked them profusely and put the card on the table. Richard leant across, read what they had written, looked up and said, 'Guys, it's only Katharine!' He meant it as a joke, but in that moment, my birthday balloon burst. What had been a lovely evening didn't feel so much fun any more. When we got home later we sorted it out (ha!), but it was a valuable lesson on the importance to me of words in our relationship and the power they have to build up … or to tear down.

A couple of years ago, I was at an annual conference and witnessed an incredible example of the potential of words to bring about change. It's a story I have come back to time and again. I had been speaking to a group of parents about the power of words and a young mum came up to me in the break and started to cry. She told me that she had two girls; the older one was a delight, but the youngest was driving her crazy:

She argues with her sister, her bedroom is a mess, she's rude and inconsiderate and she's always in trouble at school. In fact, her behaviour is causing conflict between me and my husband. We are so exasperated with her that for the last year instead of calling her by her name, 'Grace', we call her 'Disgrace'. I know it's wrong, and I'm going to go home tonight and try to do things differently.

Twelve months later, I was speaking at the same event. As I walked through the bookshop, I saw a familiar face coming towards me. Its owner was beaming and she held the hand of a beautiful little girl with curly blonde hair who, like her mum, was grinning from ear to ear. Before I could say hello to them, the mum started to speak:

I am so glad to have met you again. After the event last year, my husband and I agreed to change the way we spoke to our daughter. Even when she was behaving badly, we didn't call her 'Disgrace' but gave her her real name – 'Grace'. That one decision kick-started a number of other changes and our home is now a different place. Thank you!

Of course, the change didn't happen overnight, but that decision to speak positively was a catalyst for a new beginning. How we speak to each other in the home matters; our words are powerful.

If our spouse's love language is words, we would be wise to take extra care with what we may think are funny quips or off-the-cuff comments about cooking, driving, gym bodies or dress size, etc. They will feel them deeply. And the tone of voice in which we say things is key. 'I'll wash up tonight,' said in a harsh, resentful tone communicates something very different to exactly the same words spoken with kindness, generosity and love. We can be imaginative about showing our love through encouraging words. We can say them; we can send them by text, WhatsApp, email, snail mail, greetings cards or post-it notes; or we can put them in a lunch box, on the dashboard, on the keyboard, on the pillow or on the bathroom mirror. Words of affirmation can just be said between the two of us, or often more powerfully, in front of others.

Of course, it's important that our appreciation is genuine. Our background or personality may mean that this does not come naturally to us, but we can change our mindset and make the effort to think well of and appreciate our partner. We can intentionally seize opportunities every day to speak positively.

This isn't rocket science! – 'You look great tonight,' 'Thanks for the lift', 'Your lasagne is the best', 'I heard how well you gave that presentation', 'I'm proud of you,' 'I love you' …

… words that give life.

TIME IS OF THE ESSENCE

When Duncan and Carol bought their house they knew it needed renovating, but they were at the limit of their budget so decided that they would take their time over it; they agreed that Duncan would just go for some quick wins on a couple of the rooms. But knowing how much their home meant to Carol, Duncan set himself a secret challenge to redecorate the whole house. Visits to B&Q became an almost daily occurrence, and he worked late into the night and at weekends, sawing, hammering, painting and varnishing in order to get everything finished. He had imagined that Carol would be delighted with his progress, cheering him on, but to his surprise she seemed to become more and more distant.

The problem was that Carol's love language was time. Whilst she was grateful for his efforts, working so hard on the house meant that they hadn't had any quality time together for months and she wasn't feeling loved. All she wanted Duncan to do was to put down his tools and give her some undivided attention. Eventually, when they talked about what was going on, Duncan said that the news came as quite a relief! Finishing the house could wait for a bit.

Those whose primary love language is quality time feel loved when their husband or wife gives them their focussed attention. It could be enjoying a meal together, going for a walk, having a coffee, travelling in the car or chatting round the kitchen table for a few minutes after work. The activity itself is incidental.

'Honey, can you come here? It's half-time. Let's get some of that quality time together you keep going on about. Bring a beer while you're on your way!'

What matters is that sense of togetherness. Time is precious, and when their husband or wife gives them the gift of even fifteen minutes of their time, they feel valued, special and loved.

The digital age brings many advantages; we can build huge networks of friends and be in touch with different people simultaneously all round the world. But sometimes those connections can come at a cost. We can be globally connected to all sorts of people, but emotionally disconnected from our husband or wife – the person we love – as we text, message, tweet, blog and post. And if our spouse's primary love language is quality time, it will be especially important to take control of our environment. We all know the distraction of the ping in our pocket or on our laptop, heralding the arrival of a message to our inbox or a tagging in a tweet. But to give ourselves the best chance of connection with our husband or wife, we need to turn off the phone (or at least the notifications), put away the laptop, iPad or other electronic device, put down the newspaper, turn off the TV and give them our attention so that they know we want to be with them. Giving them our focussed attention – our time – communicates to them powerfully that they are loved.

A friend told me about a weekend away he had with his wife. He had gone to huge lengths to plan it and, after weeks of research, he booked what was advertised as the perfect romantic country hotel. Granny was enlisted to look after the children, the long-awaited day arrived and they set off in great anticipation. Alarm bells began to ring when the Google Maps lady announced that their destination was coming up on the right, despite them still being on the motorway. She wasn't wrong. The 'country' hotel was just off the motorway, and the box-like room they were allocated had an uninterrupted view of the flyover traffic.

My friend was devastated. He had put so much effort into the weekend and had really wanted it to be a memorable time (for the *right* reasons!). And as if the disappointment over the hotel location wasn't enough of a let-down, the food was disappointing and the forecast of sunshine and showers turned out to be only fifty per cent accurate – it rained 24/7. The amazing thing was … my friend's wife was perfectly happy. She didn't mind one bit about the hotel, the flyover, the rain or the food. What was important for her was spending time with him – having the opportunity to focus on each other.

When our spouse's primary love language is quality time, the chances are they won't mind *what* you do: a car journey stuck in holiday traffic, a weekend away in the rain, a meal out where the pizza tastes like cardboard – none of that will matter. What *is* important for them is that you find time – planned and spontaneous – when you can simply be together.

ACTIONS SPEAK LOUDER THAN WORDS

Showing love through our actions is about expressing love in practical ways. This is one of Richard's main ways of feeling loved. He is brilliant at DIY and a much better cook than me, but when I do practical things like sorting out the washing, cooking a meal, ironing a shirt, giving him a lift, tidying up papers, filling up the car or, on a good day, even sweeping up the leaves, it says to him: 'I love you.'

He loves surprises and in the early days of our marriage, he often arranged surprise things for me. With hindsight, I can see that in the weeks running up to my thirtieth birthday some plotting had gone on – my address book had disappeared for a short time and there had been a series of mysterious phone messages. At 7.30pm on the day itself, I came downstairs and was greeted by a room full of people – family members and friends from school, university and work. He had worked so hard to arrange the party, and I didn't want to tell him that it wasn't how I wanted to spend my birthday at all. That was a mistake, as ten years later history was re-enacted for my fortieth birthday. If I didn't want a repeat performance for my fiftieth, I realized that I needed to explain to Richard that I don't really enjoy surprises.

As we were having that conversation, I had a moment of revelation. Doing something practical – going to the trouble of

arranging a surprise for me – was Richard's way of showing his love; his love language was acts of service. I realized that if I was to express love in his love language, I needed to turn the tables and do the same for him! It was his birthday the following month and I made a plan. In a series of negotiations rivalling the complexities of Brexit, I sorted out childcare arrangements for all four children and booked to go out for the day to a place he'd always wanted to visit. The result was amazing! He was bowled over – he felt so loved – and I lived off the brownie points for months afterwards!

However, if our husband or wife's primary love language is acts of service, here is a little word of warning: if we *forget* to do something they have asked us to do it will have an especially negative impact on them.

Showing love in practical ways is not about being a doormat, but it is about spotting things – sometimes non-routine tasks – that we know our husband or wife would love us to do and doing them with kindness. Baking a cake, filling up the windscreen wash in the car, making a coffee, tidying the kitchen, changing the sheets, emptying the dishwasher, taking out the recycling, mowing the grass – all of these, if done with the right attitude, can communicate love. They generally require planning, energy, and some effort (or in my case, with one or two of these things, a *great deal* of effort!).

Showing love with practical actions won't come naturally to all of us – especially if it's not *our* main love language. The challenge is to remember to keep on doing it because when we do, we ensure that our husband or wife truly does feel loved. For them, actions really do speak louder than words.

'I got you some screen wash and an ice scraper.'

GIFTS – NOT JUST ON BIRTHDAYS

Gifts can be tokens of love and can communicate love strongly on an emotional level – it's my other love language. When we were first married, I would often save up and buy little gifts for Richard to show him I loved him.

I remember our first Christmas. I carefully planned what I was going to buy Richard, put in a huge amount of effort to get it, wrapped it beautifully in gold paper and presented it to him with a flourish on Christmas Day. I felt so disappointed when he ripped the paper off, said a quick thank you and put the present to one side. It wasn't that he didn't like the gift, it simply didn't carry the significance for him that it did for me. Over the years, we have learnt that gifts mean much more to me than to Richard, and I have needed to find different ways of showing love to him.

The love language of gifts is not about the money spent, but the thought behind the gift and the care taken in choosing it. So if your husband or wife has gifts as their primary love language, your missing their birthday, forgetting an anniversary or making a last-minute dash to Boots at 5.30pm on Christmas Eve, will be especially disappointing for them and certainly will not make them feel loved. Presentation will matter, so taking the trouble to wrap the gift rather than handing it over in a recycled Lidl bag will convey love. The best givers are those who take time to think carefully and find out what their husband or wife would like to receive.

We recently had dinner with some friends. On the way home, I commented that I had enjoyed the unusual Red Truffle hand cream in their bathroom. I loved the smell and made an extra visit to the loo as we were leaving just to use it one more time! My comment did not go unnoticed. Richard did his research and the following week a parcel arrived containing a bottle of the very same hand cream. It wasn't Christmas and it wasn't my birthday. It was a present 'just because' … and it made me feel on top of the world!

If you are not a natural spender and always want 'value for money', you may find having a spouse whose primary love language is receiving gifts a little challenging. It can also be more difficult when finances are tight. However, thoughtful gifts can still be given with little cost if a bit of creativity is involved – a handmade card, for example, a single flower or even a photograph.

For years, Simon never bought his wife Becky a birthday card as he thought they were expensive and a waste of money. After they had been married for fifteen years, they went on a marriage course and Becky told him for the first time how disappointed and unloved it had made her feel. He was mortified and resolved to make amends. He decided to send her a card every month for the next fifteen months to make up for all the birthdays he missed. It never was to do with the money, but it was everything to do with love.

We have been married for thirty-three years, and I have never taken off my wedding ring. I hadn't really thought about the significance of this until I came across this paragraph in *The 5 Love Languages*. Chapman says:

> *Visual symbols of love are more important to some people than others. That's why individuals have different attitudes towards wedding rings. Some never take the ring off after the wedding. Others don't even wear a wedding band. That is another sign that different people have different primary love languages. If receiving gifts is my primary love language, I will place great value on the ring you have given me, and I will wear it with great pride. I will also be greatly moved emotionally by other gifts that you give through the years. I will see them as expressions of love. Without gifts as visual symbols, I may question your love.[20]*

So if you are wondering whether your husband or wife's love language is gifts, their attitude to their wedding ring may just give you a clue!

Richard had been away with some friends to climb mountains in Wales. On the way home, he'd planned to buy me flowers, but it was late and most shops were closed. When they were nearly home, he asked the driver if he minded just pulling in to the local garage. Now, stocks or tulips wrapped in brown paper and tied with raffia are the flowers I love – wilting orange carnations from the garage with a reduced sticker on them would not be my first choice, and he knew that. But it was that or nothing and he bought them. When he arrived home and gave them to me

20 Gary Chapman, *The 5 Love Languages: The Secret to Love that Lasts*, p.75.

it didn't matter about them not being my favourite flowers. The fact that he had bothered to think about me and buy them said to me, 'I love you.'

Whether it's a magazine, a packet of wine gums, a T-shirt or a bunch of flowers, giving a present of some kind – and not just on special occasions – will always speak volumes to a husband or wife whose love language is receiving gifts.

Gifts are not just for birthdays.

REMEMBER THE POWER OF TOUCH

Touch communicates love more powerfully than words for some people. It says, 'You matter,' 'You are special,' 'I love you.'

Richard and I were leading a marriage event and had just introduced the next speakers. We went to sit at the back of the room. Just in front of us was a couple we had been talking with earlier. They were going through a difficult time in their marriage and had a backlog of issues that needed sorting out, but they hardly knew where to begin. They sat upright, a gap between their seats, with no sign of contact or warmth between them. But during the evening something began to change. It seems that the man was deeply affected by something that had been said. He whispered something into his wife's ear, and then I watched as, very slowly, he moved his arm and placed it on the back of her chair. She stiffened and sat still for a minute or two, and then I saw her hand reach out to touch his. He moved his hand to her shoulder and began to play with her hair. I held my breath and watched as the coldness between them seemed to melt away. Whilst I don't believe that one gesture can change everything, I do know that I witnessed that evening the amazing power of touch to communicate love in a marriage.

Alongside acts of service, touch is Richard's other main way of feeling loved. It isn't top of the list for me, and in the early

'I love holding hands with you, darling, but could we take a break
for a bit while I chop the vegetables?'

days of our marriage if I didn't hold his hand when walking down the road or didn't respond in the way he was expecting, he would genuinely feel I didn't love him. And the reverse is true, of course. So my giving him a kiss on the way out of the door in the morning, sitting by him if he's watching TV, giving him a hug rather than words of sympathy if he's had a bad day, all communicate love to him.

Just last week I was working on my laptop in our kitchen – it's the most sensible place to be because it's warm and there's a table, a chair and access to a socket. But for some reason I decided to up sticks, take the laptop into the next room where Richard was, and sit down next to him on the sofa. The effect on him of this small action seemed out of all proportion – I was amazed! All evening he kept mentioning how great it was to sit together, how he felt connected to me, how he felt loved. Whilst it remains a mystery to me, those whose love language is touch will understand how he felt.

Tom explained how he had learnt about the significance of touch in his marriage:

I didn't see physical affection modelled by my parents when I was growing up. But I have realized that for Leanne, my wife, it's important, and so for the sake of our marriage, I am trying to learn about it. It often feels awkward, but I have decided that it's worth getting over a bit of awkwardness and embarrassment in order to have a wife who feels loved.

The love language of touch covers everything from a brush on the shoulder, a hand on the knee, a kiss, a hug, a massage, right through to sexual foreplay and making love. It communicates love when it is given and a sense of rejection and isolation when it is withheld. If our spouse's love language is touch, we can discover what type of touch is most meaningful for them. Gina is married to Ethan and touch is her primary love language. She said:

> *In the last year, we have gone through a few crises as a family. Ethan isn't very touchy-feely but he has learnt that when life is tough, the very best thing he can do for me is to give me a big hug. Long after the hug is over, I will be able to remember the feeling of love and security that it gave me.*

Gary Chapman says:

> *Running the hand through the hair, giving a back rub, holding hands, embracing, sexual intercourse – all of those and other 'love touches' are the emotional lifeline of the person for whom physical touch is the primary love language.*[21]

So if touch is our spouse's love language, it's important to take every opportunity to express love in this way – not just as a prelude to making love. If it doesn't come naturally to us, as with the other love languages, we will need to be intentional. Spot those moments and seize opportunities to hold hands, snuggle up on the sofa, kiss and hug. For them, a touch makes all the difference.

21 Gary Chapman, *The 5 Love Languages: The Secret to Love that Lasts*, p.116.

VIVE LA DIFFÉRENCE!

Richard and I were visiting friends recently and decided to make a weekend of it, booking ourselves into a nearby Premier Inn. My work at Care for the Family means that I spend a lot of time in Premier Inns … I know the system. We checked in and I went into automatic pilot:

1. Find hotel room.
2. Take key out of back pocket and open door.
3. Put kettle on.
4. Unpack.
5. Hang up clothes.
6. Charge phone.
7. Put books on left-hand side of bed.

We can't have been in the room for more than a minute when I realized I had obviously not communicated this routine to Richard. He rifled through all his pockets for the key, left his suitcase on the floor, plugged in his iPad, launched himself onto the left-hand side of the bed (my side) and turned on the television. In fifteen years of staying in Premier Inns I don't think I have ever turned on the television, and for some reason I found his way of settling in (and especially the daytime TV) incredibly irritating. Of course, there was nothing wrong with his routine – or mine, for that matter – it was just *different*.

There are a lot of other differences between us as well. I like fish; Richard is a carnivore. He likes spicy food; I can't even manage a korma. He is spontaneous; I hate surprises. He watches TV to relax; I can't work the remote. He loves roller coaster rides; I like my feet on terra firma. I am people-focussed; he is task-focussed. He could find his way out of the Amazon rainforest; I can't even find my way out of John Lewis. I could go on.

The old adage 'opposites attract' has an equal and opposite maxim – 'birds of a feather flock together'. Like most couples, when we first met it wasn't the differences between us that attracted us to each other, but the things we had in common. We are generally attracted to people who have the same values and backgrounds and interests as we do – PLU (people like us). And experts agree that having similarities on the things that really matter in life makes for happiness and stability.[22] But scriptwriters would be short of material if every romcom was about a couple who had every detail of life in common, fell in love and lived happily ever after. There would be no intrigue and the plot could, dare I say, even be a little … boring.

Whilst 'like attracts like', most of us are also drawn to people who – although they may have the same outlook as us on the big picture things – have differences that complement us. Their strengths can compensate for our weaknesses and vice versa, bringing colour and vitality to our relationship. They can broaden our horizons, encourage us to try new activities or discover new ways of doing things (including daytime TV!).

But as well as bringing new experiences to our marriages, our differences also have the potential to come between us. Ben

---

22 Karl A. Pillemer, 'Opposites Attract' Or 'Birds Of A Feather' – What's Best For A Long Marriage', *Huffington Post* (31 January 2013, updated 2 April 2013), https://www.huffingtonpost.com/karl-a-pillemer-phd/marriage-counseling-opposites-attract_b_2557391.html.

loves planning – he likes nothing better than spreadsheets and colour-coded lists and his life runs like clockwork. His wife, Julie, has a more relaxed and carefree attitude to life. When they first married, he loved her spontaneity, but now he gets irritated by the chaos she leaves in her wake. Karen used to love the fact her husband, Darren, has strong opinions. As they talked long into the night on subjects ranging from global warming to the gender pay gap, she found it stimulating. Now she thinks he is stubborn and argumentative.

It's helpful to differentiate between annoying habits (which we can change) and personality differences (which we are unlikely to be able to do anything about). We have three light switches in our kitchen. Despite the fact we have lived in our house for twenty-five years, if I don't really concentrate, every time I come into the room I hit the wrong switch, so in the middle of a candlelit dinner I have the potential either to plunge people into darkness or replicate Blackpool illuminations. To Richard's (understandable) irritation, I go through this little routine most days. Someone did once helpfully suggest labelling the switch, but the truth is that, with a bit of effort and concentration on my part, this is an annoying habit that (on a good day!) I could do something about.

When it comes to personality differences between us, realistically these are unlikely to change, so we will need to be generous – and even creative – to accommodate them. No amount of effort will ever change my total lack of sense of direction. On many occasions early on in our marriage, when Richard was driving and I was map-reading, we got totally lost (with more than a little friction in the car as a result!). After a number of disastrous journeys, we learnt a better approach. If navigation became difficult, Richard would simply pull over and

'The parents get on so much better now we have two televisions.'

we would swap places. I would drive and he would map-read. No discussion needed. Job done. Peace and harmony restored. As marriages mature, many couples find they automatically adjust their behaviour to take account of their differences, bringing strength to their relationship.[23] (And, for us, Google Maps now makes life a lot easier – provided, that is, that I manage to enter the right postcode!)

So whilst the saying 'birds of a feather flock together' is certainly true, the old adage that opposites attract isn't dead in the water either. We each bring to our relationship our individual values, personalities, backgrounds and ideas of how things should be done. Whilst our similarities may have attracted us to each other in the first place, our differences can have the ability to enhance and make our marriage much stronger.

'Vive la différence!'

23 R. Gutteridge, *Enduring Relationships: The Evolution of Long-Lasting Marriage,* unpublished PhD thesis (Keele University, 2003).

'OK, it's morning. Let's get some sleep and argue again tonight.'

ARGUE WELL

The first part of a love story is the easy part. No one deserves a medal for falling in love. It is in the ensuing chapter, when differences emerge, and distress and severe upheavals disturb the dream of the relationship, that the real heroism of enduring love stories unfolds.[24]

I can still remember our first argument. Whilst I don't recall exactly what it was about (something to do with the right way to carve a chicken, I think), I do remember where we were and, more importantly, how it made me feel. We'd had the best part of a year of wedded bliss with hardly a cross word, which made this row all the more surprising. On that summer evening, I think we broke almost every rule in the book. There were raised voices (Richard), sulking (me) and misunderstandings (both of us) as the hurts of the last year all came tumbling out.

It took some time to unpick the emotions of that day – mainly due to the fact that neither of us understood two key truths: (a) that conflict in marriage is to be expected, and (b) that it is not necessarily a bad thing. The fact is that with most conflict, if we don't resolve it quickly it rumbles on; but if we do sort it out, a week later we generally can't even remember what the row

24 Janet Reibstein, *The Best Kept Secret: How Love Can Last Forever*, p.221.

was about. Conflict in a relationship is not, in itself, the problem – a certain amount can be healthy. The important thing about conflict is how we deal with it.

We each have a personal way of responding in times of conflict. Some of us can take a lot of agro and angst, we simply absorb wrongs and injustices, hurtful comments or disappointments without reacting. We want to keep the peace. Others of us can be set off by the slightest thing. We don't let anything pass, we get angry or upset – and we let you know it![25]

When marriage researchers looked into what kind of people have the best relationships, surprisingly they found that it isn't those who don't react, but those who let you know they are annoyed. They tend to have longer-lasting marriages and relationships that are happier and more fulfilled. The reason is this: rather than ignoring an issue, they flag it up and sort it out! It may have been difficult to do at times, but the issue is dealt with. In contrast, with those people who absorb all the difficulties, sweep them under the carpet and repeatedly take things on the chin, the pressure mounts inside until one day the valve gives way. When that happens, the effects can be cataclysmic!

So it may take courage, but for the sake of our relationship there may be times when, rather than sidestepping the issue, we have to face it – together.

25 John Gottman, Catherine Swanson and James Murray, 'The Mathematics of Marital Conflict: Dynamic Mathematical Nonlinear Modeling of Newlywed Marital Interaction', *Journal of Family Psychology* (1999), Vol. 13, No. 1, p.3–19.

FIGHT FAIR

Whilst watching wrestling will never be my favourite pastime, I do remember the legendary Giant Haystacks taking on Big Daddy in the eighties. At six feet eleven inches tall, Haystacks weighed in at an extraordinary forty-eight stone thirteen pounds, whilst Big Daddy sported a record-breaking sixty-four-inch chest. What was incredible about the fight (which you can still see on YouTube) is the apparent ease with which they appeared to be able to hurl their opponent's gigantic body across the ring. It was mesmerizing! But it wasn't until years later that I discovered these fights were staged. The fact that they would seriously injure each other unless there was agreement and clear ground rules had escaped me. They were not enemies – they were friends who were on the same side. They trained together to fight fair so that neither of them got badly hurt.

In the same way, there are ground rules for having a fair fight in marriage:

1. No physical violence or verbal abuse
The first and most important rule – absolute and non-negotiable.

2. Step into the ring
Depending on our personality, some of us will find conflict more challenging than others. If we find it difficult, our default position may be simply to keep the peace. Instead of dealing

with the issue, we sidestep it or resort to passive aggressive tactics. For instance, we won't tell our partner if we're upset or cross with them; we expect them to read our minds – to pick up the cues or to know anyway. Or perhaps we give them the silent treatment, sulking or withdrawing emotionally. However, if there is an issue between us – something that needs resolving, it is generally so much better to face it and deal with it. Researchers have found that the happiest couples accept that arguments (even recurring ones) are inevitable, but see them as opportunities to understand each other better.[26] So the general rule is that the issue will only be resolved if we step into the ring – and for many that can take courage.

3. Remember you are on the same side

When conflict comes between us, it creates a 'Me v You' situation. We marshal our weapons, entrench our positions and before we know it we are mounting an offensive by land, sea and air. But it is so much better to remember that in marriage we are on the same side. We can call a truce, lay down our weapons and put the issue out in front of us so we can tackle it *together*.

4. Attack the issue not the person

When he left the house that morning, Ross had every intention of going to Freddie's parent-teacher evening, but at 6.20pm a crisis at work took his attention. The next thing he knew it was 7.30pm and Janis, his wife, was on the phone, angry, disappointed and let down. She had every right to be mad with him, and he apologized and promised it would never happen again. Whilst he soon got over missing the appointment, what

26 Janet Reibstein, *The Best Kept Secret: How Love Can Last Forever*, p.48.

was more difficult for Ross to recover from was Janis' comment (admittedly made in the heat of the moment): 'You're a rubbish husband and a hopeless father.'

It's vital when we're dealing with conflict to remember that there's a difference between arguing about the issue and criticizing the person. Two little phrases that make it personal and can so easily slip out in the heat of the moment are, 'You *never*' and its first cousin, 'You *always*': 'You never put a new loo roll on when it's finished,' or 'You always check your phone just when we go to bed.' It's important to let each other know if we feel strongly about an issue, but these two little phrases simply add fuel to the fire. Instead, we can say how it makes us feel: 'I feel like you take me for granted when you leave it to me to replace the loo roll,' or 'It makes me think that the phone is more important to you than I am when we're in bed.' Expressing how the problem makes us feel means that we don't point the finger at our spouse and, more importantly, leaves room for the possibility of change.

5. Listen to the full story
An easy mistake to make when having a disagreement is not letting our partner finish what they are saying and jumping to conclusions before we have heard the full story. There might be a good explanation for what has happened. Listening shows respect and helps us to grasp the heart of the problem so that we can resolve it together.

6. Be prepared to lose an argument
Richard and I both trained as lawyers. We were taught how to build a watertight case, how to assemble facts for a successful prosecution and how to mount an irrefutable defence to both

'I know I'm right, but I'm going to pretend that you're right. OK?'

judge and jury. Whilst these persuasive skills are useful in a court of law, they are not helpful to bring into a marriage – winning will never be as important as it seems. Both of us can be tenacious (aka stubborn), and in an argument we can find it challenging to back down. We recently disagreed over an issue, both convinced we were right, and we reached an impasse. That was until I remembered something a friend had once said to me: 'Katharine, sometimes you need to lay down your right to be right.' Although it was not what I wanted to hear at the time, she was wise.

This is not about one person always giving in, but about both being prepared to lose the argument occasionally for the sake of the marriage.

One other caveat, if we are always determined to win – and particularly if we are the one who is quicker with words – is that whilst we may have the joy of victory, we may eventually end up being the loser. If our partner has not been able to articulate their point of view, they may be left with a lot of pent up emotions. Even if they keep a lid on them for the time being, we should beware … they will almost certainly come out one day, maybe when we least expect it.

Conflict comes to every marriage – both small inconsequential issues and bigger ones that can go to the heart of the relationship. But agreeing some basic ground rules and learning to fight fair means that rather than damaging our marriage, our disagreements can actually strengthen it as we work through them together. The main issue isn't about whether there are a couple of sarcastic comments or a barrage of full scale rows but *how* – and more importantly *if* – we make up afterwards.[27]

---

27 Aaron Anderson, 'Why Fighting is Good in Your Marriage', *The Marriage and Family Clinic* (15 July 2014), http://themarriageandfamilyclinic.com/why-fighting-is-good-in-your-marriage/.

'Don't let the sun go down while you are still angry,'[28] a little verse often quoted at weddings, is good advice for couples to sort out arguments before they go to bed. Of course, if we are tired and emotionally exhausted that may not be wise to take literally – the principle is to resolve the issue as soon as we can. Richard and I have tried our best to heed that recommendation, but I also like the idea behind a well-known quote: 'Don't go to bed angry. Stay up and fight!'

28 Ephesians 4:26, NLT.

FIND THE THIRD WAY

If you read any agony aunt column, you will soon find that the agreed wisdom for settling disagreements in marriage is to opt for compromise: put the other first, put your marriage above your personal agenda, give up your rights and let your husband or wife have their way. It's not bad advice – it keeps the peace and solves the issue – but it is a bit passive. It can mean that although we end up with something that we can both live with, it's very much second best.

Philip Jinadu speaks about this subject at Care for the Family's marriage event *It Takes Two*, and I love the example he gives from his own marriage. He says:

> *When Kate and I married, it wasn't with the intention of having the world's greatest compromise. I want something better, something special, something inspiring.*
>
> *In our marriage, one of our biggest areas of conflict has been about how we decorate our house. When we were first married, we discovered that we had wildly different tastes in decorating. Somehow this hadn't come up in the marriage preparation course we did! Kate loves things that are floral, expressive, romantic and Laura Ashley. Whereas my style is understated. It's chic, it's minimal, it's modern, it's elegant, it's cream, it's chrome – it's Jasper Conran and it's happening!*

When we came to decorate our first house, we realized we had a problem. Kate took the initiative – she was amazing. She gave me carte blanche and let me decorate the first room my way – exactly how I wanted it. It was understated, it was chic, it was minimal, it was modern, it was elegant, it was cream, it was chrome – and it was happening. I was thrilled. It was the spare room. As soon as it was done, she produced her trump card. She said, 'Now that we've done the spare room your way, it's only fair that we do our bedroom my way.' She set to work and soon there were roses, vines and creepers growing all over the walls. As I lay in bed, I didn't know whether to go to sleep or to get out the secateurs and do some gardening! I had been out-manoeuvred. How could I have been so naive?

The house ended up looking like it was at war with itself. It was, in a sense, a picture of how we did marriage. Compromise. Your way, then my way, your way, my way. And very often that's how marriages carry on. Tit for tat. You get your way, now I get my way. It's fair and equitable. But it's not very exciting.

Eventually we moved house and we began decorating again – your way, my way, your way, my way – until we realized we had made a grave error. We'd bought a house with an odd number of rooms! After some discussion, we came up with an idea. Instead of compromising, we decided to see if we could find a third way. Not your way, not my way, but our way. We would take my best ideas and Kate's best ideas, and then we would combine them to see if we could create something that's uniquely us. It wouldn't just be floral and it wouldn't just be minimal, but a combination of the two. We set to work on the final room

... and that is how floral minimalism was born! And it's by far the best room in the house.

This story illustrates how marriage can be. It's not simply about compromising, but about having synergy – working together to do something that is more than the two of you could do on your own. Philip continues:

I didn't marry Kate so that I could impose my will on her, and she didn't marry me so that she could dominate me with her style. So we tried applying that principle to the rest of our lives. We bring the best of her and the best of me, we talk it through and we see if we can find the third way. We try to do family life and parenting our way. We try to do our budgeting and finances our way. We try to do the in-laws, holidays, Christmas, leisure times, our love life together, our way.

After we'd been doing this for a while, we began to discover that although it takes more effort, there's almost always the ability to find a third way. So when there is conflict between us, we try to remind ourselves that it's an opportunity for us to do something even better. It's not just you and it's not just me, but it's 'us'.

One of the important characteristics of successful marriages is for the couple to have a strong sense of togetherness and identity as a couple.[29] Finding the third way achieves a good balance between having our individual needs met and strengthening our 'coupleness'. It doesn't mean that the relationship is more important than our individuality, but that our sense of being a couple enriches us as individuals.

29 Jeanette Lauer and Robert Lauer, *'Til Death Do Us Part* (Routledge, 1986).

'I don't think there is a third way to make toast.'

There are three essentials for finding the third way:

1. We need to take our time

It's much easier to do what we normally do and what we know how to do, but when we want to find something brand new, we'll need to give it some careful thought. We are going to have to experiment sometimes, face up to the fact that it might not always work at first, and have another go. It will take longer, but the result will be worth it.

2. We need to talk it through together to find out what we both want to do and why

It's important to ask each other what we are trying to achieve and what values are behind it. When we've done that, we can talk about how we can combine the two things into something brand new that we've never done before.

3. Finally, we have to trust one another and respect each other's opinion

It doesn't work if one of us is just trying to manipulate the other person so that they can get their way anyway. We need to trust that both of us will lay down our rights and our agendas and genuinely find some common ground. And, in that process, we will create something brand new – something that we have generated together *as a couple*.

It's easy for marriage to turn into a bit of a battleground. We all know people who are entrenched in their positions – it's their way or the highway. But it's hard to have a deep relationship with somebody like that. Our well-worn paths look safe and right to us, but if we work at it, we can sometimes find that other path. It's not so well trodden, but it's full of possibilities – our third way.

'I feel like something has come between us.'

STOP – OR ELSE!

Perhaps it is not surprising that one of the most stressful times for a couple is after the birth of their first child. They are adjusting to a demanding new role as parents, whilst suffering from long-term sleep deprivation at the same time. A little person who needs attention 24/7 and doesn't know the difference between night and day has suddenly come into the relationship.

Let's Stick Together is a popular course by Care for the Family that gives new parents some great relationship skills. Many couples have told us that one of its most helpful ideas is the concept of STOP signs.[30] But understanding STOP signs can make a difference to couples in *any* marriage, not just new parents.

The STOP signs are simply four bad habits that many of us easily slip into, particularly when tired or stressed:

S – *Scoring points*
T – *Thinking the worst*
O – *Opting out*
P – *Putting down*

30 The STOP signs are based on 'Danger Signs' as discussed in Howard Markman, Scott Stanley and Susan Blumberg, *Fighting for Your Marriage: Positive Steps Preventing Divorce and Preserving a Lasting Love* (Jossey-Bass, 1994).

'I said I'm fine.'

Scoring points

When we feel criticized or under attack we may be tempted to return fire. But trying to score points off each other can intensify the issue unnecessarily, turning a simple comment into World War Three.

Imagine the scene: Dave comes in from work and notices that Jo hasn't taken out the recycling.

Dave: 'I thought I asked you to do that this morning.'

Jo: 'I didn't have time. I had to call into Sainsbury's because you forgot to go yesterday.'

Dave: 'I didn't go to Sainsbury's because you asked me to call in on your mother to fix her fridge.'

Jo: 'Well, I've just spent at least half an hour on the phone sorting out *your* mother – and she wants to come for Christmas.'

Dave: 'At least that will be easier than having *your* mother to stay.'

Within seconds, and frighteningly easily, a fairly small niggle over recycling has developed into an issue about their relationships with Jo's mother.

Trying to get the better of each other only escalates a difficult situation. We need to STOP scoring points!

Thinking the Worst

Another bad habit is automatically thinking the worst. In marriage, it might show up where a harmless action or comment makes us think that our partner is getting at us or that we've done something wrong. For some of us, it's practically in our DNA, but it *is* a habit that we can stop.

Rewind the scenario above: Dave comes in from work and notices that Jo hasn't taken out the recycling. At the same time, he receives a text reminding him of a difficult meeting tomorrow that he has forgotten about. He sighs and takes the recycling out. Jo hears the sigh and – thinking the worst – assumes he is mad with her for forgetting to do it herself. Her mood spirals down and she becomes defensive. The evening doesn't go well and Jo goes to bed believing that Dave blames her for not getting things done, whilst he has completely forgotten about the recycling but wonders what on earth he's done to upset her.

Jumping to negative conclusions undermines trust in the relationship and is a bad idea. If it's an ingrained habit, we may have to purposefully challenge ourselves, but for the sake of our relationship we need to STOP thinking the worst!

Opting Out
Opting out involves withdrawing from the situation, switching off or shutting down.

Back to Dave and Jo: Dave comes in from work and notices that Jo hasn't taken out the recycling. He is mad with her as she also forgot to do it last week, but he hates confrontation so simply takes the box outside himself. Jo knows he is annoyed and there is an atmosphere between them. Later on, she asks him what's wrong and although he's fuming inside, he replies, 'Nothing,' and shrugs and walks away.

Refusing to deal with a problem is another bad habit. Whilst things may seem fine on the surface, it is difficult to resolve an issue with, or get close to, a person who has left the room or simply withdrawn emotionally. We need to STOP opting out.

Putting Down
A put-down involves words or behaviour that give the impression that we think we are better than the other person. It could be a comment or even a gesture.

Back to Dave and Jo one more time: Dave comes in from work and notices that Jo hasn't taken out the recycling. He raises his eyebrows.

Dave: 'Jo, you are hopeless. Wednesday night equals recycling night. How difficult can it be?' He picks up the box, shakes his head, and walks out of the door.

Saying things that are disparaging or belittling, or doing something to humiliate or embarrass our husband or wife are incredibly destructive to our relationship. We need to STOP putting each other down now.

Becky has been married to Liam for four years. She commented:

> *Understanding the STOP signs has been brilliant for our relationship. Looking back, we realized that between us we had every single one of these bad habits. I tended to score points and put down, and Liam would think the worst and opt out. I'm not sure we will ever manage to get rid of them completely, but we are trying and it has made a massive difference to our marriage.*

'Are we ever going to talk about the "you know what"?'

KEEP SHORT ACCOUNTS

We were recently at a friend's wedding. We had sung a rousing hymn, the couple had made their vows to each other and we had just settled down for the address. They had asked a retired bishop to speak, a man we loved and admired, and we were looking forward to him sharing some of his great store of wisdom. To our surprise, he began by giving the newly-married couple some practical advice. He said that when they came home from their honeymoon they should return their new super king-sized bed (a wedding gift from their parents) to the shop and get a smaller one. Of course, his recommendation was tongue-in-cheek, but he said that it was based on that wisdom from the Bible I mentioned in a previous chapter: 'Don't let the sun go down while you are still angry'(or in more modern parlance: 'Resolve the flack before you hit the sack'). Why? Because with a smaller bed, there was less chance of being able to cling onto the edge with a wall of hurt and anger between them.

Many years ago, I remember coming home from work to find a neighbour sitting at the kitchen table with Richard. We had exchanged pleasantries over the years, but as I sat down with them, I realized there was more to his visit than a discussion about the broken fence or overhanging tree. His head was in his hands and through his tears, he told us that he had come home that evening to find a note from his wife pinned to the kitchen noticeboard. She had left him and she wasn't coming back.

There was no warning and no explanation. She had simply …
gone. They had argued that morning about the dog, but he said
it was nothing major. Stirring his tea, he kept repeating the same
phrase: 'Why didn't she tell me? I just didn't see it coming. I just
didn't see it coming.'

Some marriages collapse because of a tsunami of a crisis –
a breach of trust, a financial disaster, an affair. But others fail
simply through the incremental build-up of layer upon layer of
minor hurts and grievances that have been left unresolved. In
his book *Falling*, journalist John Taylor describes the breakdown
of his eleven-year marriage.

> *'We have to separate,' my wife told me. It was a late-
> summer evening eleven and a half years after we had
> gotten married. We were on our deck, drinking gin-and-
> tonics and smoking cigarettes, an entitlement of marital
> stress …*
>
> *'We do?' I asked. After all, our marriage wasn't hellish,
> it was simply dispiriting. My wife and I didn't hate each
> other, we simply got on each other's nerves. Over the years
> we each had accumulated a store of minor unresolved
> grievances. Our marriage was a mechanism so encrusted
> with small disappointments and petty grudges that its
> parts no longer closed.*[31]

It seemed that this, too, was our neighbour's story. A litany of
annoyances, upsets and hurts had built up over the years, and
on that June day, one more irritation about a wiry Yorkshire
terrier had simply tipped the balance – and it was over.

31 John Taylor, *Falling: The Story of One Marriage* (Ballantine, 2000), p.3.

In marriage, it can be so easy to let those minor frustrations and grievances build up, but it doesn't have to be that way. Instead we can try to keep short accounts – which first means being honest with each other when we have been hurt. All of us, at times, have either deliberately or unintentionally hurt each other. We may think it is obvious that our partner has upset us, but none of us are mind readers, and there will be occasions when we need to spell out to our husband or wife that we are feeling hurt.

Jim, who has been married to Zoe for ten years, said this:

My parents divorced when I was young, and I didn't want to repeat their mistakes. I was terrified of conflict and so never told Zoe when I was hurt or annoyed. I just buried it and hoped it would go away. I genuinely thought that was the right thing to do. But I found not dealing with the issue just made me feel more annoyed with her. Because I didn't tell her she had hurt me, she had no idea. Things eventually came to a head, and I now make a point of saying when I am hurt. I realize our relationship can handle it, and it's so much better to have everything out in the open.

If we know we have hurt our husband or wife, the next step is to apologize and ask for their forgiveness. With Richard and I, that is something we don't always find easy!

We were leaving the house slightly later than planned for a family party, so my blood pressure was rising – we didn't want to reinforce our already well-earned reputation for arriving late. I was waiting by the car and Richard came out wearing a shirt that I hadn't seen before. For reasons best known to myself, I chose that moment to make a comment on his colour coordination and fashion sense: bad move. The shirt really wasn't *that* awful; he liked it, and being critical about it when we were already late was not the most thoughtful or kind thing to do. We set off in stony silence down the M4. I knew I should apologize but pride got in the way – after all, I reasoned, he often commented on what I was wearing and, anyway, the shirt just didn't look good – it was the wrong colour and too small.

I am ashamed to say that this internal debate went on for some considerable time. I played a game in my head: 'I'll say sorry at the next motorway bridge … or maybe the next one … or perhaps the one after that.' Eventually, when we reached Reading, sense prevailed and I said sorry. The effect was astonishing; the atmosphere in the car changed immediately! If only I had apologized as we left the house we'd have had a far more pleasant car journey.

Now that may be a trivial example, but the principle is the same for big issues as well. Acknowledging when we have been hurt and have hurt each other, and then apologizing, can take courage. We may need to swallow our pride, but doing so opens the door to the possibility of forgiveness and reconciliation. Hurt will come to every marriage. Be the first to say 'Sorry'. As Ruth Bell Graham wisely said that a happy marriage is the 'union of two good forgivers.'[32]

At the beginning of this book, I quoted a passage often read at weddings. It contains a little phrase that packs a big punch: 'Love … keeps no record of wrongs.'[33] Intimacy in marriage is built on trust, and trust is built on openness. But it's hard to be open with each other when we have unresolved hurts. If we are harbouring a grudge, or feeling resentful or hurt, we are

32 Ruth Bell Graham, *It's My Turn* (Billy Graham Evangelistic Association, 2007).
33 1 Corinthians 13:1,5.

more likely to close down and not share our hopes and fears. To restore closeness in our marriage we need to bring our hurts into the open, apologize and forgive each other.

Forgiveness doesn't mean that we have to pretend it hasn't happened – but it may sometimes mean that we choose not to take offence. I love this story from the book I wrote with Rob Parsons, *The Really* Really *Busy Person's Book on Marriage*:

> *On her golden wedding anniversary, my grandmother revealed the secret of her long and happy marriage. 'On my wedding day, I decided to choose ten of my husband's faults which, for the sake of our marriage, I would overlook,' she explained. A guest asked her to name some of the faults. 'To tell the truth,' she replied, 'I never did get around to listing them. But whenever my husband did something that made me hopping mad, I would say to myself, 'Lucky for him that's one of the ten.'* [34]

We can hurt each other over small issues – a sarcastic comment, a thoughtless action, a forgotten anniversary – and, of course, there can be deeper hurts that go to the very roots of a marriage. In my role at Care for the Family, I see enough pain in one week to last a lifetime, and I know that there are no easy answers. I also know it is not possible to save every marriage. Nevertheless, I often also see men and women who are trying with every fibre of their being to unleash the power of forgiveness in a marriage.

One couple, Claire and Steve, told us their story. Every time I tell it, it brings me encouragement and hope. They met when they were teenagers and became good friends. Claire went

34 Rob Parsons and Katharine Hill, *The Really* Really *Busy Person's Book on Marriage* (Muddy Pearl, 2016), p.25.

'Just filling in the fight book for our records.
What started this one?'

to London to college. Steve followed and, shortly after, they married. When Steve got a job in a recording studio, it involved him working night and day, seven days a week. Neither was happy with the situation, but they didn't know how to address it. Steve was totally involved in his job and Claire became disillusioned and deeply unhappy. They told me what happened next:

Claire: Someone else began noticing me, giving me time and attention, and I fell for him. Then one day he gave me an ultimatum. He was leaving his marriage and wanted me to do the same. I felt trapped and didn't see any alternative. I jumped ship.

Steve: I just didn't see it coming. It was the most painful experience of my life. I knew I didn't want our marriage to be over, and I told Claire that I would fight for her.

Claire: I was hurting and had pinned all my hopes and my future on this decision. But after two weeks, the man I was with had a change of heart. He said he needed to go back to his wife to try to make things work. I felt embarrassed and humiliated. Without thinking, I picked up the phone and called my best friend, the person I had known longest in my life – Steve. It was the way he responded that gave me hope for our marriage.

Steve: I was determined that our marriage wasn't going to be another statistic, and I wasn't going to let it go without a fight. I remember reaching a crossroads in my thinking: I could very easily slip down the path of bitterness and unforgiveness, and wallow in it, or I could choose to forgive and dare to trust again. That has been the biggest journey. People talk about earning trust, but for me trust was a choice. I had to get to the point where I was prepared to put my heart on the line. It's not been easy, and it was a daily choice to be prepared to risk it all again.

Claire: Steve was gentle and gracious. Incredibly, he allowed us to talk about our feelings without showing any bitterness. We had counselling and, together, we were able to unpack our brokenness and the hurt of the past and make a new start. It has been a hard journey but, looking back, we would say to any couple facing difficulty, 'Be honest with each other and be gentle. There is always hope.'[35]

I will never forget speaking to a woman at one of our events whose husband had had an affair. She had two small children and was deeply hurt, and I was so moved as she shared her story. I knew there were many things she wanted to talk to me about, but early on she said these incredible words: 'I am trying to forgive him because I know that if I don't forgive, I'll be the one that's in chains.' She had, perhaps, come across the old saying: 'The one who cannot forgive must dig two graves.'

Unforgiveness casts a long shadow, not only across the relationship we have with the person who has wronged us, but across our own lives as well. Forgiveness enables us to move forward without being weighed down by the past. The woman continued her story: 'I realized that time alone wouldn't heal the hurt – only forgiveness can do that. What helped me was

35 Claire shares more of her and Steve's story in her book: *Taking Off the Mask*. Claire Musters, *Taking Off the Mask* (Authentic Media, 2017).

my belief that God had forgiven me, and I knew I could allow that forgiveness to flow out to others.' That didn't mean that she didn't stop feeling the pain. But she recognized that forgiveness wasn't about her feelings, it was something she could choose to do. In her case, it was a choice that she made every day. A choice to let go.

And when the hurt is deep that is a costly thing to do. Rob Parsons writes: 'Forgiveness feels the pain, but doesn't hoard it; it allows tomorrow to break free of yesterday. It is always hard, sometimes foolish and, at its heart, God-like. There is no hope for us without it.'[36]

---

36 Rob Parsons, *The Sixty Minute Marriage*, p.45.

'We're going to have to move that last one
to next week again, I'm afraid.'

A SLOWER DAY
NEVER COMES

An ancient book of wisdom reminds us that: 'There is a time for everything ...'[37] In the busyness of family life, however, it can be tempting to think that the author simply got this one wrong.

'How are you doing?'

'Good, thanks, but busy. How about you?'

'Busy too – but doing well!'

Sound familiar? I seem to have this conversation if not most days, certainly most weeks. 'Busy' has become a cultural badge of honour that most of us wear with pride. Diaries are filled in half-hour slots, whether with work engagements, children's schedules, doctors' appointments, gym classes or coffees with a friend. We have apps that track tasks, deadlines, calories, the number of steps we take and how many hours of sleep we need. Our 24/7, always-on, multi-tasking lifestyles have blurred the lines between work and home. We live in an uber-society – a society in a rush. We have more time-saving devices than any previous generation, but seem to have less time. We are running to keep up on a treadmill of busyness. And what for?

Whilst busyness may give us a (dubious) sense of purpose and significance – and may even be a defence against feeling

37 Ecclesiastes 3:1.

that life is trivial or empty – it can chip away at the things that are most important in our lives. Some things can be done in a hurry, but relationships take time, love takes time, and our marriages can so easily become the casualty of our over-busy, over-stretched lifestyles.

Richard and I were recently speaking at a conference. In one of the breaks, we spoke to a young man. He was married with three young children. His job meant that he had to work unsociable hours and was often away from home. His wife was trying to set up her own business, which was taking her time, energy and attention. Their children needed to be taken to school and ferried between a never-ending programme of after-school activities. They were engaged in their church and local community. They wanted to spend time with extended family ... the list went on. They were running to keep still and their marriage was beginning to feel the strain – they were like ships passing in the night.

We chatted over coffee and, although there is no silver bullet we could give him, we did share a couple of insights that he said were helpful.

1. Realize that a slower day never comes

Rob Parsons writes about what he calls 'The great illusion':

> *You can run several agendas in life, but you cannot run them all at a hundred percent without somebody paying a price ... We have so many excuses. The main one is that we convince ourselves a slower day is coming. We say to ourselves, 'When the house is decorated, when I get my promotion, when I've passed those exams – then I'll have more time.' Every time we have to say ... 'Not now, darling,' we tell ourselves it's OK because that slower day is getting*

nearer. It's as well that we realize, here and now, that the slower day is an illusion – it never comes.[38]

2. Consider how we value time

I was recently challenged to look at time differently – it's not about how much time has passed, but about valuing it because of how we use it. I discovered that this simple poem gave me a different perspective.

To know the value of one month, ask the mother of a premature baby.

To know the value of a week, ask the writer of a weekly blog.

To know the value of a day, ask the dad who sees his children on Saturdays.

To know the value of an hour, ask the young man waiting for his fiancée to call.

To know the value of a minute, ask the teenager who just missed the last bus home.

To know the value of a second, ask the driver who just avoided the accident.

To know the value of a millisecond, ask the athlete who won the silver medal.

38 Rob Parsons, *Loving Against the Odds: Creating the Marriage You've Always Wanted* (Hodder & Stoughton, 2005), p.23.

There are 1,440 minutes in a day and we each choose how to spend them. Let's not kid ourselves that we are simply in a busy 'season'. That slower day never comes. We need to make time for things that are important and for the people in our lives that are important – to make time for our marriages. And we need to make it now.

MAKE A DATE

Instead of just focussing on how many minutes we can carve out in our busy schedules, we can think about what we would like to accomplish in that time. When we do that, we often discover that we have more time than we realize.

One of our projects at Care for the Family involves helping dads who are in prison with their family life, and we spoke recently to Corin Morgan-Armstrong who has pioneered the incredible Family Interventions programme at Parc Prison in Bridgend. Perhaps unsurprisingly, research has shown that the stronger the relationship that the prisoners have with their families whilst they are in prison, the less likely they are to reoffend. As well as giving parenting support, Corin has spent time helping prisoners make the most of the limited amount of contact they have with their partners. Relationships are often strained and, during visits, he noticed some couples just sitting there in silence, not knowing what to say. Since then, he has encouraged the men to be proactive about visiting time – to think ahead and write down what to talk about. It's a simple exercise that has transformed visiting time and strengthened the couples' relationships. Those sixty minutes have changed from being an awkward and painful endurance test to the best hour of the month.

These men have learnt to make the most of the little time with their partner that they have. Yet in many marriages,

'I can do 12 July next year, but it will have to be a lunch date. Does that work for you?'

where couples are living under the same roof and sleeping in the same bed, they hardly spend even one hour of meaningful time together. A recent UK poll found that a third of couples spend less than thirty minutes a day of quality time together, and three in ten feel their relationship is suffering due to the lack of 'couple time'.[39]

Diane Sollee, a pioneering psychologist in marriage education says: 'Love doesn't commit suicide. We have to kill it. Though it often simply dies of our neglect.'[40] Despite best intentions, many marriages can slip into what is known as 'a creeping separateness'. When our four children were little, there was a period when this happened to Richard and me – it wasn't a decision we made, simply a way of life we had drifted into. At that time, my focus was the home, and my day involved the toddler group, Play Doh, the missing hamster, jam tarts, the school run, spellings, bath time, story time and bedtime. Richard's day at the office looked a little different. It was taken up with appointments, interviews, meetings, phone calls, business lunches, finance, strategy and five-year plans. We began living parallel lives.

It might have gone on like that for some time, but some wise friends encouraged us to make a few changes – namely to plan to have regular time together. That advice was life-saving! Since then we have made the effort to spend time together each week, and it has helped us reconnect at a meaningful level. We have had to be flexible and have needed to make adjustments to make it work in the context of the different seasons of family life that we have gone through. When the children were at primary

39 Kyrsty Hazell, 'Couples Spend Just Thirty Minutes a Day Together, Study Reveals', *Huffington Post UK* (30 November 2011) https://www.huffingtonpost.co.uk/2011/11/30/couples-spend-just-30-minutes-a-day-together_n_1120721.html?guccounter=1.
40 Diane Sollee, Marriage Quotes, *Smart Marriages* (Accessed 19 June 2018). http://www.smartmarriages.com/marriage.quotes.html.

school and I was at home, we would meet each other for a coffee or lunch. After I was back at work and when the children were teenagers (and often out and about!), Friday nights worked better.

Spending planned time together – a date – doesn't have to be complicated or cost a lot of money. It could be an evening at home with a ban on technology and DIY, seeing a film or going on a picnic, for a walk or a drink. It is simply time together doing something fun that we enjoy. These occasions weren't – and aren't – always wonderful and romantic; there have been a few disasters! And sometimes there has been a run of weeks when we didn't manage it. But the important thing is that, more often than not, it happens. Our date night (or morning or afternoon) gives us the opportunity to step off the treadmill of busyness and invest in our marriage. And over the years it has paid dividends.

There are three things that have to be in place if a date night is to happen:

1. Plan

We have discovered that we need to put our date night in the diary in the same way as any other appointment, usually several weeks ahead, otherwise the rest of life simply takes over and time together is squeezed out. When I used to meet Richard at lunchtime, he put it in his work diary. If a client wanted to see him, he would tell them he was busy – he had a prior meeting. And at that particular season of life, that made me feel valued and special.

2. Prioritize

There will always be other (often appealing) things that will challenge our time together. If we have put a date in the diary for Friday night and a friend asks if we can meet up, nine times out of ten we will say 'No.' We don't necessarily have to tell them we are 'just' seeing each other. Prioritizing it above other things underlines how important it is to us and to our marriage.

3. Protect

We need to be prepared to defend our time together! Our experience is that the minute we have agreed the time, a zillion other unplanned, 'urgent' things appear on the horizon demanding our immediate attention. Protecting our time means doing our best to be ruthless and put aside all interruptions (including our phones!).

As well as a planned hour or two together, many couples have discovered the benefit of a longer time away – a night or even a weekend. Childcare, health or finances can make that a real challenge, but where possible, it's a great investment. Richard and I didn't go away together when our children were little. This was partly because I thought we would be overburdening grandparents or friends in asking them to help out, and partly because I thought that we were letting our children down in some way. Actually, nothing could be further from the truth! If you have children, one of the most positive things you can do for them is to invest in your marriage. Researchers have found that married couples who go on occasional date nights have 14% lower odds of their relationship breaking down,[41] and Sir Paul Coleridge, Chairman of the Marriage Foundation, said: 'Enjoying your relationship is the best thing you can do for

41 'Date Nights Make for Longer-Lasting Relationships – But Only if You're Married', *Marriage Foundation* (25 September 2016). http://marriagefoundation.org.uk/date-nights-make-for-longer-lasting-relationships-but-only-if-youre-married/.

your kids. And date nights are surely the really fun part of that responsibility. Neglect your relationship and your children are the biggest casualties.'[42]

All four of our children have (in theory!) left home now, but although we have more time on our own, we still find we can take each other for granted, so planning a fun, relaxing time together regularly continues to benefit our marriage.

For all of us, whatever season of marriage we are in, we need some one-to-one time. So click on your calendar, open your app or your diary and make a date!

42 Ibid.

HAVE FUN!

Laughter is good for us, and it's also good for our marriage. When we speak to couples who are going through a dry time in their relationship, one of the things we usually ask them is when they last had fun and laughed together. Very often they will look at each other and give a wry laugh because it hasn't happened for ages. Life can be challenging and there will be seasons when we are simply in survival mode. When demands on our time pile up, it's the fun in our relationship that can easily fall by the wayside. But even in the tough times, taking time to laugh together and not take ourselves too seriously is a good thing. Researchers have found that there's a significant link between fun and a happy marriage,[43] and that's because the intimacy of sharing light-hearted moments together strengthens the bonds between us.[44]

When the book of Proverbs was compiled, it included the well-known saying: 'A cheerful heart is good medicine',[45] and 3000 years later, science agrees. Laughter is good for us. Research shows that when we laugh, the tissue that lines our blood vessels expands. This increases blood flow and improves the health of our arteries. One cardiology professor shared a simple

43 Sharon Jayson and USA Today, 'Married Couples Who Play Together Stay Together', *ABC News* (16 July 2008). https://abcnews.go.com/Health/Family/story?id=5387217&page=1.
44 Robyn Parker, 'Why Marriages Last: A Discussion of the Literature', *Australian Institute of Family Studies, Research Paper No. 28* (July 2004).
45 Proverbs 17:22.

'Come here a minute, dear. I think I've figured out a way to laugh more.'

prescription for a healthy vascular system: 'Thirty minutes of exercise three times a week and 15 minutes of laughter on a daily basis.'[46]

Happily married couples say that humour is one of the most important bonds between them.[47] By 'humour' they generally mean something deeper than the latest jokes or memes doing the rounds on social media. It is more about the way they relate to each other with low-key, kind, spontaneous joking, laughing and bantering that keeps them connected.

Helen and Jon reflected on their marriage of thirty-five years:

We have demanding jobs and are quite serious people, but when we are together we do try to have fun. Jon is a great storyteller, and I sometimes think he spends most of the working day planning how to make me laugh when he comes home at night. Having that attitude stops our marriage becoming boring and mundane. It means we don't take each other for granted.

Bestselling novelist Jilly Cooper would agree. When she was asked the secret of her fifty-two-year marriage to her husband Leo, she said: 'It's bed springs creaking from screaming with laughter – not from sex … Sex is wonderful, of course, but I think it's finding things that amuse you.'[48]

Having fun together will look different for different couples – practical jokes, funny stories, YouTube clips, a comedy box set

---

46 Hara Estroff Marano, 'Laughter: The Best Medicine', *Psychology Today* (9 June 2016). https://www.psychologytoday.com/us/articles/200504/laughter-the-best-medicine.
47 Judith S. Wallerstein and Sandra Blakeslee, *The Good Marriage: How and Why Love Lasts*, p.202–3.
48 'Jilly Cooper: 'Love is bed springs creaking from laughter and not sex', *Belfast Telegraph* (14 September 2016. https://www.belfasttelegraph.co.uk/life/features/jilly-cooper-love-is-bed-springs-creaking-from-laughter-and-not-sex-35046421.html.

or laughing about 'disasters' such as baking a cake for the school fair with salt instead of sugar or the smart dinner he attended wearing a jacket with the '75% off' tag clearly visible. At other times, it will defuse and bring perspective to a difficult situation. As I am writing, a familiar ping has just announced an incoming WhatsApp message. A friend has sent me a photograph. With a blizzard raging outside, her doorbell had just rung and she had opened the front door to be greeted by her husband dressed up in a snowman onesie, complete with coal buttons and eyes and a carrot nose. Yes!

I was having coffee with a friend the following day and as we laughed at that photo she reflected that although, at the start of our marriages, we want good-looking husbands who are sexual athletes and great at DIY, a little later in life many of us would gladly settle for a man who loved us enough to make us laugh and turned up on our doorstep with coal buttons and a carrot nose.

LOVERS NOT FLATMATES

Richard and I love helping with marriage preparation courses. Last Tuesday night was no exception. Emma and Connor arrived early and we enjoyed hearing all about their plans for the big day. Connor was the champion of the list and his master spreadsheet took no prisoners. Confetti and cars, flowers and favours, banns and buttonholes, vicars and veils – all had been marshalled and arranged in colour-coded sequence. After a bowl of pasta, we moved swiftly and seemingly effortlessly from chatting about the choice of hymns and colour of the bridesmaids' shoes to life beyond TBD (the big day).

This was the second evening we spent with them and we had already talked about the subjects of communication, the influence of family background, spending time together and conflict. All of these were a necessary foundation for that night's subject: sex and intimacy. Emma glanced at the diamond on her left hand and looked up at Connor. They smiled knowingly; like every newly-engaged couple they were in love – truly, madly, deeply – and they knew their sex life would be uncomplicated and glorious. Whilst they realized that they might need some conflict-resolution skills now and again in the arena of domestic chores, their sexual relationship would be different – tender and intimate, exhilarating and magnificent. But for now they would humour us.

No matter how long we have been meeting with couples in pre-marriage counselling, when it comes to the subject of sex and intimacy we are often met with the same response – even if it's unsaid: 'That's one area you don't have to worry about!' But the truth is that whilst sex can be one of the most fun, enjoyable and satisfying parts of marriage, with incredible potential to draw us together, it can also be fraught with difficulties and disappointment. Like every other area of marriage, it doesn't just happen; it needs work. It takes good communication, time, sensitivity and generous hearts that are open to discovering and meeting each other's needs.

Whether we are teaching about marriage at a large event or running pre-marriage counselling in our home, we share the following lessons (many of which we wish we'd learnt ourselves a lot earlier!):

1. It's not just you

In 1885, a firm which manufactured cosmetic soaps made a discovery: sex sells. They started to put trading cards in their packaging which included erotic images of the day's most popular female celebrities.[49] The connection between sex and soap was somewhat tenuous but, in terms of increasing sales, it worked and, ever since, brands have purposely linked themselves to suggestive sexual imagery in the search for new customers. Sex sells deodorant, chocolate, cocktails, cars and holidays in the sun – everything apart from, ironically, baby products. But although sex is everywhere, most of us still find it a difficult subject to talk about in the context of our marriages.

Our sex life is a deeply private and personal area where we are at our most vulnerable. It involves openness and trust, and we may need to overcome shyness or inhibition. We may find it

49 Paul Suggett, 'Does Sex Really Sell in Advertising?', *The Balance Careers* (3 January 2018). www.thebalancecareers.com/does-sex-really-sell-38550.

difficult to talk to each other – let alone to others – and this can lead to a feeling of isolation.

Richard and I had just finished speaking at a marriage event. Most people had left the auditorium, and the team began clearing up stray leaflets, packing away books and stacking chairs. I looked up and noticed a young couple hovering nervously by the back wall. They had waited until everyone else had left and now tentatively came forward. The husband thanked us for the evening, but I waited as I sensed there was something more. Eventually his wife spoke, her voice just above a whisper. She said: 'In so many ways, we've got a good marriage. It's just that we have real problems with our sex life.' With his wife having had the courage to begin the conversation, the man joined in and the hurts, disappointments and challenges they had experienced all came tumbling out.

The truth is that most marriages go through times when sex is not so great (in fact, research shows that it's normal in long-lasting relationships for there to be sexual troughs).[50] It could be in the early years of marriage, after the birth of a child, during stressful times at work, the menopause or for no obvious reason at all. Over the years at Care for the Family, we have talked to thousands of couples about this subject, and they consistently say one thing. It goes something like this: 'It's such a relief to know that we aren't the only ones who are finding our sex life difficult at the moment … that it's normal … it isn't just us!'

2. We live in the real world

Sex scenes in Oscar-nominated films almost always portray couples as young, toned and beautiful. They leap into bed with

50 Janet Reibstein, *The Best Kept Secret: How Love Can Last Forever*, p.8.

mutual excitement and reach simultaneous heights of passion at a moment's notice. Crisp, white Egyptian-cotton sheets flow off the bed, pink roses are on the bedside table and there are no shopping lists, dental floss or phone chargers in sight. Muddy trainers, baskets of washing or wet towels to trip over are nowhere to be seen. The women are stunning with legs to die for and perfectly made-up with not a hint of smudged mascara. The men are tanned, with a gym body and designer stubble. And the sex is long, lingering and glorious.

It's as well that we realize from the outset that, in our sex lives, we don't need to compete for an Oscar. Sex is part and parcel of normal everyday family life. We live in the real world, and in the real world bedrooms get untidy, children stumble in at just the wrong moment, there are periods and pregnancies, tiredness and stress.

Our sexual relationship is a complex dance that we learn over time. Whilst we may hear of couples who boast of having orgasmic sex two or three times a day – and most likely half the night – for most of us, what matters is not about frequency or even technique. It is about finding a pattern of intimacy that works for *us* in the particular season of marriage that we are in.

And to do that, we need to communicate.

3. Communication
Although it's not easy, learning to talk about our sexual relationship together at a level we are comfortable with can help us build closeness and intimacy together. It may feel awkward, but even beginning by telling each other what we find enjoyable (and what we don't) can be a start. Communicating how we each feel and what our different needs are can make a big difference.

4. We are all different

Assumptions that are based on generalizations about men's/women's attitudes to sex can be unhelpful and no marriage is a stereotype. Many couples find they have differing levels of desire, so what's important is to understand ourselves and our partner, and to discover what works best for *us*.

But whilst it's not helpful to make generalizations, there are often some common differences between men and women. Although it's not true for everyone, one of these is that men tend to become aroused much more quickly than women. Someone once described it like this:

> *Men can't get enough sex; women can't get enough romance. Men are thinking about the destination; women are thinking about the road. Men are like gas cookers: they heat up instantly and cool down rapidly. Women are like electric cookers: they take time to heat up but stay hot for much longer.*

The scenario could easily be reversed, of course, however, most men can be at death's door with a raging temperature, barely able to reach for the Lemsip, but the moment their wife puts so much as a toe under the duvet … zing! Instant recovery!

But we are all different and each marriage is unique, therefore understanding our husband or wife is an important step in being able to meet each other's needs.

5. It's about the relationship

When counselling couples at Care for the Family, we often ask them if they could change something in their marriage what that would be. Now of course, there are marriages where the wife will want sex more than her husband, nevertheless it is more common that a man will say: 'It would be for my wife to want sex more often. I would like her to initiate sex.' We turn then to the woman and ask the same question. Invariably, her answer will be along these lines: 'I'd like him to be more affectionate,' 'I wish he would hold my hand when we're out rather than walk ten yards ahead,' 'I'd like him to notice my hair,' 'I'd like him to touch me without it always having to lead to sex,' 'I just want to know that I matter.'

For many women, sex is more complex and is bound up in the relationship as a whole. So for there to be a good time of lovemaking, conflict needs to be resolved, they need to feel cherished and they need to feel safe. One woman said, 'I feel connected through intimate conversation and he feels connected through sex. I need intimacy before sex; to him intimacy *is* sex.' The mind also plays an important role for women. Often, simply making the choice to engage, to give or to respond when feeling tired or apathetic can mean that the feelings then follow.

And for men, the key to a better sex life can simply be to make sure that a woman knows that she matters. As someone once put it: 'The greatest erogenous zone in a woman's body is her heart.'

6. Keep a sense of humour

Keeping a sense of humour was something we needed to remember on our honeymoon. We arrived at our destination – a hotel where the rooms were in little stone bungalows in beautiful gardens – and in great anticipation, leaving a trail of confetti, we carried our cases through an avenue of beautiful purple flowers to our allocated room. Diamonds danced on the sea as it glistened in the distance, and it felt like the perfect start to married life. But as we opened the door to the room, any dreams of long nights of glorious sex came to an abrupt end. Our 'honeymoon suite' consisted of two rock-hard single beds that were at least five feet apart. They were also built into the stone wall, so there was no hope of even dragging them together. In that moment, we discovered that an essential part of developing a good sex life was not to take ourselves too seriously. And, hey, it was our honeymoon ... so we managed!

7. The barometer

We have a barometer in our hall that tells us, with varying degrees of accuracy, what the weather is doing outside. We can look to see whether the sun is shining or whether snow, hail and sleet are on the way. In the same way, our sex life can indicate what is happening in our marriage. Kirsten reflected on this as she spoke of her relationship with Ryan:

We have really noticed how what is going on in our daily lives impacts our sex life. When Ryan was going through a tough time at work, when the children were little and didn't sleep, when they were teenagers out late and we hadn't yet heard their key in the door, or when either of us was feeling stressed, irritable or unwell, then sex seemed to be off the agenda. I suffered from postnatal depression after our second child was born, and our sex life seemed to be on hold for ages, which I know was frustrating for Ryan. But he was so kind and understanding. And there were times when he found stress at work affected his sex drive, and I had to be especially affirming with him.

'I'm just finishing up our schedule ...'

The season of marriage when there are young children, which often coincides with a demanding time in the workplace, can be exhausting. Many couples collapse into bed at night and are just too tired for sex, with feelings of either frustration or guilt in abundance. For that reason, our sexual relationship, particularly at this point in our marriage, sometimes needs a little extra time and attention.

8. Time

Simply having time for sex makes a difference. Sex is easier when we aren't rushed and can take time to unwind. We can focus on each other and don't have other issues demanding our urgent attention. Our sex life can be harder to nourish in the middle of a busy lifestyle and, of course, to the long list of things which have always affected the bedroom – pressures at work, worries about money as well as children knocking on the bedroom door – there is now the added killer of digital intrusion. A recent report showed that 7% of people actually check their phones during sex![51]

As much as our instinct is that sex should always be spontaneous, in order to counteract the busyness of our lives, sometimes it is no bad thing to plan for sex – or at least for the possibility of it. One couple we know distinguish between 'gourmet sex' (when there is plenty of time) and 'quickies' (when there isn't). Anna says:

Although we would love to always have 'gourmet sex' on the menu, for all kinds of reasons we know that's not realistic. Having said that, we don't want our sex life to

51 iPass Mobile Professional Report 2017. (Accessed 19 June 2018).
https://www.ipass.com/research/ipass-mobile-professional-report-2017/.

*become mechanical and routine, so we have learnt to try
to make room for both!*

Another couple reflected:

*I know it sounds a bit clinical, but life is so hectic we found
that if we didn't plan ahead, we were just too tired for sex.
So we set aside certain nights at least for the possibility of
sex. I'm not saying it will work for everybody, but we have
come to regard those nights as special. Of course, it can still
happen spontaneously, but we're beginning to see the value
of taking our sexual relationship seriously.*

9. Help is at hand

When we walk into the bedroom at night, we are not just
bringing ourselves, but the history of our lives. We have a past
that has influenced our understanding and our expectations.
The messages our parents gave us as children, our experiences as
adolescents, our love lives as adults – these experiences all shape
us into the people we are now. We may come to our marriage
with a wide discrepancy in our sexual experiences, and there
may be physical or emotional difficulties to overcome. I have
often spoken to couples who have gone through incredible
challenges – including, for some, the trauma of sexual abuse.
For others, illness or disability means they may not be able to
make love in the way they had hoped, but they have found new
ways of expressing physical intimacy together that have brought
them closer and strengthened their marriage.

In our experience, many difficulties can be overcome just by
bringing them into the open and talking them through together.
Sometimes, though, we can be facing problems that need expert

help. So if you have issues that you haven't been able to sort out together, find someone you trust to talk to. (See Appendix for organisations offering support.)

Whilst our marriages won't stand or fall by the quality or quantity of our lovemaking, we are meant to be lovers not flatmates. Sex is an important part of marriage and it's worth taking the time to invest in.

'Go upstairs and make love, you say?
Darling, I can do one or the other...'

THE TEN-SECOND RULE

I have many memories from my time as a family lawyer but one in particular sticks in my mind. Jan's story is not unique – in fact, it is representative of many men and women who sat in that same chair in my office over the years. She began by telling me about the Friday morning she would never forget. Her husband was going to a conference, and after dropping the children at school she had offered to give him a lift to the station. She pulled up outside the Co-op so he could run in to pick up a sandwich. He had left his phone on the passenger seat and while she waited for him, a familiar bleep indicated that a text had arrived. She glanced sideways to see who it was from and picked up his phone. As she read the message, time seemed to stand still. Her stomach lurched and it felt as if the air had been sucked out of her lungs. She saw her husband coming out of the shop, sandwich in hand, and hurriedly put the phone back on the seat. Fighting back the tears, she tried to pretend nothing was wrong. She needed space to think – to recalibrate her world. When he returned home the following day, she confronted him and the whole story of his affair came out. And now here she was, sitting in a lawyer's office, her ten-year marriage in pieces.

In our work in Care for the Family we have spoken to many people who have had affairs, and so often they will say that they never intended to be unfaithful to their partners: 'It just happened.' The truth is that in many ways it is easier than ever to slip into a relationship outside of marriage.[52] Digital technology has increased the opportunity and many are now having 'virtual affairs' via their chat app of choice. A smartphone in the pocket is all that's needed to make it happen.

One husband discovered that his wife had been chatting to a married father of three on WhatsApp several times a week. They were engaging in intimate conversation and exchanging explicit photographs, all whilst he was at work or asleep next to her in bed. According to a recent survey of 27,000 people, twenty-three per cent said they felt that their desire for infidelity would be satisfied with a relationship conducted purely online, without ever meeting the other person face-to-face.[53]

Opinion is divided as to whether a virtual affair is the real deal, but it does involve the same emotions – secrecy, excitement, fantasy, rationalization and denial of consequences. And, although the online experience is enough for some people, for most it's not. Unsurprisingly, they often lead to a desire to meet in real life. So whilst the internet may have blurred the lines, affairs of the heart – virtual or otherwise – continue to destroy trust and destroy marriages.

But before we become complacent, it's good to remind ourselves that affairs generally don't begin with sex; they start because of emotional involvement over intimate conversation and time together. Looking back, those who have been involved in an affair will often talk about some innocent event that began it all – often a genuine desire to help someone. One thing led to another and, somehow, the relationship got out of control. With

---

52 'Online Affairs Can Be Addictive, New Study Finds', *Science Daily* (1 October 2015).
https://www.sciencedaily.com/releases/2015/10/151001130303.htm.
53 'Are Online Affairs OK?', *Askmen*. (Accessed 19 June 2018).
https://uk.askmen.com/dating/dating_advice/online_affairs.html.

some, it wasn't so much that they were looking for an affair; it was more that the affair found them.

Sharon had been happily married to Colin for seven years. She was working on a project with another man at work and, to her surprise, she found herself attracted to him. Her marriage was fine, she loved Colin, and so she was taken aback by the suddenness of her attraction and the strength of her feelings for him. A friend at work made a passing comment about how well they seemed to work together, and this chance remark was the wake-up call she needed. Whilst she realized she couldn't help being attracted to him, she knew that she could choose not to act on it. She asked her employer if they could be put on different assignments in future. She had no idea whether her colleague had any feelings for her, but acting quickly when she had the first warning signs had pulled her back from the edge of the cliff.

One man described what he called the 'ten-second rule'. He remembers being at his work Christmas party and being stuck in a boring dead-end conversation with the Sales Director. As he looked across the canapés for a means of escape, he caught the eyes of a colleague he'd chatted to the previous week and who he found attractive. She smiled. He knew there was chemistry between them. He said:

I had ten seconds to decide whether to cross the room. And in those ten seconds I decided to walk those thirty feet towards her. We chatted for hours that night, and a few weeks later, we began a physical relationship. I left my wife and two small children. It didn't last long, but my wife won't have me back. I miss them. I often think back on the ten seconds that began it all.

Whilst that one text, phone call or message doesn't constitute an affair, it is frequently the beginning of a connection that secretly grows. The text spirals to a phone call, and then a lunch date and then a drink in the evening. We'll convince ourselves that we can stop it at any time but, so often, we can't. I have been involved in family counselling for over thirty years, but I am still staggered at the pain that can be brought to husbands, wives, children and often a host of others because of those ten seconds.

It takes ten seconds to pick up our phone and invite someone to lunch; ten seconds to text someone and offer them a lift; ten seconds to look them up on Facebook … just ten seconds.

THE PRICE OF THE AFFAIR

In almost every affair I have seen, the same three things will happen. The first is that those involved start behaving completely out of character. Friends ask if they are having a midlife crisis. Strongly held personal convictions are tossed aside, they buy more fashionable clothes, change their taste in music, start to wear jewellery, take up new hobbies – in fact, almost everything about them is different. Secondly, people will try to rewrite the history books. They say, 'Looking back, I'm not sure we ever really loved each other. We were so young. We were never really happy.' It's as if the dazzle of the affair plays a trick on the mind and blinds them to every memory of love and happiness.

If that's the first two characteristics of an affair, then the third is close on their heels. It may come within a few weeks or could take a few years, but real life will suddenly announce itself loudly and clearly. For a while, the thrill of the affair, the secrecy and passion, is new and exciting. But then things begin to settle down. Conversation is no longer scintillating, sex isn't always thrilling, the kitchen needs decorating, the car needs a service and the bills still have to be paid. The old adage is true: 'The other person's grass may look greener, but it still needs mowing.'

Maybe there is a loss of contact with children. We think we've dealt with that, but one day we wonder what they look like first thing in the morning and what it feels like to be able to kiss them goodnight as they go up to bed.

At the beginning of the affair, the price tag reads: 'Free'. We kid ourselves that it's fine, no one will mind, it's OK to spend a little time together. But as things progress, it's as if there's a sales assistant at the back of the shop whose job is to change that price tag. All of a sudden, it costs us something. The affair now calls for some economy with the truth: 'Sorry I'm late – work drinks,' 'Must be a wrong number – how strange.' But who cares? We tell ourselves it's the price we have to pay in order to be with someone who listens and pays us attention … and the sex is amazing. And then comes the line that clinches the deal. We say to ourselves: 'This is the person I should have married.'

Then one day we notice something that knocks the breath out of us. The price tag has changed one last time. It reads: 'Everything'. We try to argue with the sales assistant – to bargain with her – but it seems there's no leeway. We gasp with shock. We can't possibly pay this without losing all that we have built our lives on – our husband, our wife, our children, our home, our friends and sometimes even our job.

War journalists often report on collateral damage caused during fighting – innocent victims who have been hurt, maimed and injured unintentionally as they get caught up in the conflict. There is probably nothing quite as effective as the affair for causing collateral damage in marriage. Those involved are so often blind to the tragedy they have unleashed that will cause heartache not just to themselves and their children but to wider family, friends and beyond. The devastating effect of divorce and separation on children is now well-documented, and they carry the scars well into adult life.[54]

54 A. Mooney et al, *Impact of Family Breakdown on Children's Well-Being: Evidence Review*, (London: Department for Children, Schools and Families, June 2009), p7.

In my work with families, I have seen many marriages survive the trauma of the affair, but even in those situations, most people I've spoken to who have been involved in one look back with regret. One woman said to me:

I wish I could turn back the clock. If I could, I would put better boundaries in place. I thought I was in control, that I could stop it, but I didn't realize I couldn't until it was too late. I wouldn't have secrets – online and in real life. And most of all, I wish I hadn't taken my husband and our marriage for granted.

Of course, our marriages go through tough and often boring times. We dream of fresh excitement and romance. But I am sobered by a famous line written by George Bernard Shaw. He could have been speaking of the affair: 'There are two tragedies in life. One is not to get your heart's desire. The other is to get it.'[55]

55 George Bernard Shaw, *Man and Superman: A Comedy and a Philosophy* (Westminster Archibald Constable & co, 1903), Act 4.

BEWARE THE BIG LIE

A letter to a husband:

I am leaving you. Our marriage looks so good from the outside – we have good jobs, two great kids, a lovely home and a good social life. But I have decided that I can't go on with it any more. Our family and friends will be shocked and upset, and I will tell them that we have simply drifted apart. Except that isn't the truth. It is your addiction to porn that has slowly but surely driven a wedge between us. It has almost destroyed me. You preferred the downloads – the fantasy images – to me … and it has made me feel worthless.

You don't know this, but in the early days of our marriage I remember tidying your desk and finding your magazines in the bottom drawer. I was shocked, but I put it behind me – after all, what was the harm? But I was wrong. I didn't realize how it was the start of something that would take hold of you; something that would grow roots to entangle you and eventually wind themselves round the very heart of our marriage.

After the girls were born, I noticed you became less interested in sex. I blamed myself. My flabby, post-baby, breastfeeding body was two stone heavier than on our wedding day and the sleepless nights had taken their toll. I dieted, joined a gym and worked hard to regain my pre-baby weight. I think I didn't do badly at this, but nothing between us changed. I just wasn't good enough. Whenever we made love there was no tenderness or affection; it felt like you were disengaged, going through the motions, your mind on other things. Overall, though, we got on well enough. And I wanted to make it work – not only for our sake, but for the sake of the children.

Technology brings the women of your dreams to you. With your laptop on your knee and your smartphone in your pocket, you can indulge in them at any time and in any place – at work, on the train, even in our bedroom. I have grown resentful of the 'time out' you need when you come in from work or the extra half-hour downstairs before you join me in bed. I have learnt to turn a blind eye, but I know what you are doing.

I have come to the painful realization that I will never satisfy you. I will never be enough. I can't compete with the digitally enhanced, always-pouting, ever-inviting, always-on women whose company you keep. They seem to ask nothing from you. But they have actually taken everything … including our marriage.

Research tells us that pornography has cast a dark shadow over many marriages. Those who watched porn were twice as likely to divorce in the following years as those who hadn't.[56] And

56 'Beginning pornography use associated with increase in probability of divorce', *American Sociological Association* (22 August 2016). http://www.asanet.org/press-center/press-releases/beginning-pornography-use-associated-increase-probability-divorce.

porn is not just the preserve of men: women are becoming increasingly as likely to view porn.[57] Whilst there is nothing new about pornography, what has changed in recent years is that unregulated free content can be seen on digital devices at a speed, and on a scale, that previously wasn't possible. A recent study of people aged between eighteen and thirty-five found that 73% of women and 98% of men reported internet porn use in the previous six months.[58]

I recently heard a heartbreaking interview with a young man called Matt. He had started to watch porn at fifteen and, in order to satisfy his increasing appetite over the years, he began looking at more explicit content. At university his porn habit continued – along with a series of failed relationships with girls. Shortly after university he married, but as a couple they had problems in their sexual relationship. He believed his inability to maintain an erection was a physical problem and went to see his GP. The medication he was prescribed only made things worse. He then went to see a counsellor who suggested he watched porn with his wife to try to overcome his issues – advice they didn't follow.

Matt explained what happened next:

I was desperate. Eventually, I was referred to a therapist who diagnosed 'porn-induced ED (erectile dysfunction)'. I couldn't believe what she was saying. She explained that over the years, watching porn had conditioned my brain to be aroused only by seeing sexual images on screens, and it had left me unable to be aroused by my wife. At the

57 Amanda De Cadenet, 'More Women Watch (and Enjoy) Porn Than You Ever Realized: A Marie Claire Study', *Marie Claire* (19 October 2015). https://www.marieclaire.com/sex-love/a16474/women-porn-habits-study/.
58 M. Daspe, et al, 'When Pornography Use feels Out of Control: The Moderation Effect of Relationship and Sexual Satisfaction, *Journal of Sex and Marital Therapy*, (2018), Volume 44.

> *time, with all my friends watching porn, it seemed a simple*
> *pleasure, and I didn't think there was anything wrong with*
> *it. It's only now that I understand the damage it causes.*
> *Porn kills intimacy.*

Matt and his wife have now received the help and support they needed but his story is not unique. Angela Gregory, a psychosexual therapist at Nottingham University Hospital, commented that over the last ten years, she has seen an increasing number of couples presenting with sexual difficulties that have their root in porn and chat room use.[59]

Five Reasons Why Porn Is a Bad Idea for Your Marriage

1. Porn is addictive.[60] Pleasurable activities (such as watching porn) cause the brain to release dopamine – the chemical responsible for reward and pleasure. Repeated dopamine surges mean that the brain becomes desensitized to its effects, so after time a bigger dopamine hit is needed to produce the same feeling. In the same way that long-term drug users need more and more drugs to experience a high, so those using porn need more stimulation to achieve the same effect.

2. Porn is isolating. It begins in secret and traps users in a web of secrecy. They confess to feeling shame about watching it in the first place and to experiencing an added layer of shame about hiding it from those they love.

59 Simon Mundie, 'Easy access to online porn is 'damaging' men's health, says NHS therapist', BBC Newsbeat. (15 August 2016). http://www.bbc.co.uk/newsbeat/article/37058019/easy-access-to-online-porn-is-damaging-mens-health-says-nhs-therapist.
60 V. Voon, et al, 'Neural Correlates of Sexual Cue Reactivity in Individuals with and without Compulsive Sexual Behaviours', *PLOS 1*, Vol. 9, No. 7 (2014). http://journals.plos.org/plosone/article?id=10.1371/journal.pone.0102419.

3. Porn can mask other problems. Whilst it may seem to give a short-lived, dopamine-fuelled buzz or feeling of connection, over time consumers can become more depressed, socially isolated and anxious than ever.[61]

4. Porn is me-focussed and results in unrealistic expectations for real-life relationships. It gives the message that sex is a performance that is divorced from relationship, consent, respect, faithfulness and commitment.[62] Marriage is about giving, but porn allows us to have sex on our terms with an always-available, always-ready partner. It doesn't require tenderness, patience or understanding; it isn't dependent on affection and closeness.

5. Porn kills intimacy. It sabotages the ability to enjoy sex with our spouse by creating a visual route to orgasm that is unmatchable in the real world. A healthy sexual relationship in marriage is the culmination of the closest, most loving, tender and intimate connection possible between two real people. But porn has exploited sex in such a way that it has become an impersonal, solitary act of masturbation while watching fantasy images.

If porn is an issue in your marriage, know that you aren't alone. Be courageous, confide in a friend and seek help. There are organisations offering support not just for the person with the addiction but for the partner as well. (See Appendix.)

At Care for the Family, we receive emails most weeks from those struggling with porn in their marriages. And whilst it is

61 'Why Watching Porn Can Make You Feel More Isolated, Depressed & Lonely', *Fight the New Drug* (28 April 2018). https://fightthenewdrug.org/porn-can-make-you-more-depressed-and-lonely/.

62 N.M. Lambert, et al, 'A Love That Doesn't Last: Pornography Consumption and Weakened Commitment to One's Romantic Partner', *Journal of Social and Clinical Psychology*, Vol. 31, No. 4 (2012), p. 410–438. https://doi.org/10.1521/jscp.2012.31.4.410.

not easy, time and time again we see couples facing up to these issues together and finding resolution.

One husband said this:

> *I first started watching porn when I was a teenager. It didn't seem to be a massive deal at the time, but I came to realize that it was threatening my family relationships – especially my marriage. The hardest part was admitting that I had a problem and telling my wife. But we were able to get help and support. I now understand some of the reasons why porn had become such a habit. It is a journey that we are on together, but I am no longer living with the secrecy and shame of porn. We are hopeful for a new beginning in our marriage.*

'A new beginning.'

FIND HELP ON THE JOURNEY

Marriage is an adventure – an adventure not without its challenges – and there will be times in each of our marriages when we need some help along the way. In fact, sociologists have found that 'couples with a greater proportion of shared friends are happier in their marriages',[63] and that they 'not only derive great enjoyment from their friendships with other couples but are likely to appreciate each other more.'[64] This doesn't mean that we have lower expectations of intimacy and friendship in marriage, simply that we recognize that it's unhealthy to expect to get all our needs met by our partner. Our marriage should certainly be our *primary* relationship, but not our only one.

Friends are also important to a marriage because we need people we can be real with and people who will give us help when we need it. Richard and I are fortunate to have had a number of good friends over the years, some of whom we have known from the early days of our marriage, and we know that they have our backs.

Two friends in particular fulfil that purpose for us (and much more). On one level we have much in common whilst on

63 Geoffrey L. Greif and Kathleen Holtz Deal, *Two Plus Two: Couples and Their Couple Friendships* (Routledge, 2012), p.29.
64 Ibid, p.3.

'We know what it's like, we had the same issue. It took
twenty-three years for Fred to remember to put the
toothpaste top back on, but it was worth the effort.'

the other we are polar opposites, but our friendship has grown and deepened over the years. We try to support each other not just in life but in our marriages, and we've shared in each other's joys and happiness, challenges and pains in equal measure. This hasn't just 'happened' – we've needed to be intentional about keeping this relationship going. Although it's not always possible, we try to meet up once a fortnight. We eat together, laugh together (lots), cry together (too often) and drink the odd glass of wine together. But these friends have been more than simply two people with whom we spend time socially. They have been a powerful force in supporting our commitment to each other, encouraging us to have fun, to laugh and to spend time together but also spurring us on to face up to and work through the challenges Richard and I have encountered as a couple. They have played a vital role in enjoying the good times, helping us through the tough ones and saving us from slipping up. And we hope we have done the same for them!

Whilst friends are important, Richard and I have also had help from a little higher. We were at a wedding last month where, to the bemusement of the congregation, the person marrying the couple produced two bits of string and a length of fishing line. He twisted the string and fishing line together and then read a beautiful piece of ancient wisdom from the book of Ecclesiastes: 'Though one may be overpowered, two can defend themselves. A cord of three strands is not quickly broken.'[65] He explained that the two bits of string represented the bride and groom and that they were stronger together than apart. But the presence of the third strand – which represented the power of God – made an even greater difference in their marriage.

65 Ecclesiastes 4:12.

I think that church leader was right. Of course, your beliefs may be quite different, but Richard and I believe that marriage consists of the emotional, physical and spiritual. Making time for that last part has been key for us. In both the good and the most testing times of our relationship, we have prayed together and been able to draw on a power higher than our own.

The journey of marriage is made much easier if you are able to seek friendly guidance and support. There's a lovely saying about the good things in life, including friendship: 'If you have a few good friends, food on the table, and a roof over your head, you are richer than you think.' I agree!

LEAVE AND CLEAVE

Nick was pleased when his parents found a flat for him and his new wife Jess – just down the road from them! Jess wasn't so sure, and alarm bells rang when her mother-in-law, Louise, mentioned she'd had a key cut to keep 'for emergencies'. Jess's fears were not unfounded. She liked Louise enormously, but she couldn't handle coming home from work to find her sitting at the kitchen table chatting to Nick. When Louise offered to make her a cup of tea, Jess couldn't help feeling irritated – 'It's *my* kitchen.' Whilst Louise's intrusiveness was annoying, what she found even more difficult was the closeness of the relationship Nick still had with his mother. Jess felt bad admitting it, but she was jealous. Nick would tell his mother everything about his day as soon as he got back from work, and Jess resented the fact that she didn't get to hear it first. By the time he got round to telling her it was old news.

Jess had every right to feel annoyed. When we are married, our first loyalty needs to be to each other. We begin life completely dependent on our parents, but as we grow up this needs to change. We are on a journey to independence, and marriage marks an important stage in the process as we step back from our parents and build a new bond with our partner. This doesn't mean we have to take a job in Boston or trek across the Australian outback – it is about emotional rather than geographical closeness. You can live next door and have made

'I took the chance to re-arrange the living room while you were out, it was all wrong. It's alright, dear, you don't have to thank me. I'll get on to the bedrooms next.'

that separation, yet have moved to Timbuktu and still have those ties.

The shift away from parents and into marriage is part of the wedding ceremony in Western religions. One of the most moving moments of our daughter's wedding service was when we symbolically passed her hand to Will, our new son-in-law. (And, yes, we both shed a tear.) In the Jewish ceremony, the bride and groom stand under a *chuppah* – a canopy hung over four poles which symbolizes the new home that they will build together.

Family life is complicated and relationships can be anything but straightforward, so it can take time for newly-married couples to make that transition. It can be even more complicated if parents have been divorced and remarried, as there are extra people involved and more potential for misunderstandings and conflicting loyalties. When we have a close relationship we need to loosen the ties to that person, and they need to step back and allow us to make a new centre of gravity in our home.

Thankfully, Nick realized what an effect his mother's interference was having on their marriage and, to his credit, he took action in time. He put some boundaries in place that included insisting that she let them know before coming round and that she used the doorbell rather than her key. Nick commented: 'I have always been close to my mum, and it was a difficult conversation, but once I understood how it was making Jess feel I knew I needed to say something. It was tricky, but it was worth it.' Jess commented, 'I was so grateful to Nick for listening to me and tackling it before things got out of control. It meant we could manage his mum's expectations together, rather than it being something that came between us.'

The flip side of making that separation is the opportunity

to then build a new mutually supportive relationship with our parents. They can be a great source of encouragement, help and friendship, especially if children come along. We know couples who had difficult relationships with their parents growing up, but whose marriage has been a great healer. It has enabled them to make a new start and build the relationship on new terms.

Marriage experts Nicky and Sila Lee give some wise advice: 'For the sake of your parents, keep in touch. For the sake of your marriage, keep in control.'[66]

---

66 Nicky and Sila Lee, *The Marriage Book: How To Build a Lasting Relationship* (Alpha International Publications, revised edition, 2003), p.194.

LOOK BACK TO MOVE FORWARD

Family life can be complicated and whilst dealing with family ties is important for first marriages, there are even more issues to take into account in the case of a second marriage. Instead of breaking with the ties from our childhood, we need to separate from the emotional attachments of our previous marriage.[67]

Whether a first marriage has ended in divorce or because a husband or wife has died, it takes time to deal with the emotional ties that we still have with our partner. Even if a marriage has ended acrimoniously, we will still have had hopes and dreams for that relationship which need to be left behind. When we have been divorced, we begin our second marriage hoping that it will be different this time, but it is inevitable that we will face challenges of some kind. When this happens, we should be aware of the tendency to sometimes view the first marriage through rose-tinted spectacles, rather than as it actually was.

Remarriage after bereavement raises some different issues. As we build our new relationship, it doesn't mean that we should 'forget' the past one. Birthdays, anniversaries, Christmas, children's milestones and family occasions can all be painful reminders that someone you loved deeply is no longer here

67 Judith S. Wallerstein and Sandra Blakeslee, *The Good Marriage: How and Why Love Lasts*, p.290.

to celebrate and be a part of them. Our friend Howard was widowed after ten happy years of marriage to Caroline, and recently married again. This is a paragraph from an email he sent reflecting on his relationship with his new wife, Megan:

It's probably inevitable that I make comparisons, but they are dangerous – partly because every marriage is different and also because of the danger of hurting Megan's feelings. I think if your first marriage was happy, the power of nostalgia can make it seem even better than it was … The wound of bereavement cuts deep, but over time it begins to heal. Remarriage can be part of the healing process. Whilst the scar has faded, it will never go away completely. It is thirteen years since Caroline died, yet a couple of weeks ago, I heard a piece of music that reminded me of her and it left me in tears. With it came the sense of disloyalty to Megan. Of course, it wasn't unreasonable of me to have felt like that, but it was good to be able to share it with her and receive her understanding and support.

Many second marriages will mean a new family life that involves children from one or other partner's previous relationships. Whilst step-parenting is often a joy, there can also be difficult issues to deal with. Kathy was a single parent for a number of years and has now remarried. She spoke to me about the challenges of marriage in a blended family:

Being in a blended family is not for the faint-hearted. It is marriage for the marines! Whatever the circumstances that have led up to the journey into this uncharted territory, there will be challenges to face. All the aspects of the first marriage, including how it ended and especially any children, now affect our new marriage. It's therefore important to be gentle with each other and give ourselves time to readjust. There may be issues of trust and commitment which come to the surface when we least expect it, and there will inevitably be times when we misread each other. The history and complicated web of relationships with stepchildren and ex-partners means that we need to give ourselves slack. And we also need to try extra hard with all the things we know we need to do in theory, but which are so hard to put into practice – things like listening to each other, affirming each other and being open about our struggles. Date nights have been a lifesaver for us. Building a marriage in the context of a blended family takes courage and patience, but the rewards are huge!

It is inevitable that we will be affected in some way by our past relationships. For some of us they will have been a force for good in our lives, and for others a source of hurt and grief. But whatever our circumstances, we need to acknowledge those past attachments in order to move on in our new marriage – we need to look back to move forward. I love Janet and Ellis's story: they met at a divorce recovery group and both had children from their previous marriages. They have now been married for nearly twenty years. It has not been without its difficulties, but Janet refers movingly to a memory she had when she suddenly realized that their second marriage felt firmly in place. I love how she put it: 'It was no longer just a temporary shelter from the storm,' she said. 'It was a safe harbour for the rest of our lives.'

'This new budget software requires the new iPhone – we're all going to have to get one.'

DISCOVER THE MONEY SECRET

Many years ago, I was involved in running a legal advice centre in a deprived area of Bristol ('centre' is a bit of a misnomer as legal advice and assistance were, in fact, dispensed from a tiny caretaker's room at the back of a local school, which inexplicably always smelt overpoweringly of raw onion). Each Thursday evening, we would offer free legal advice to anyone who turned up.

Nine out of ten cases involved money or, more specifically, debt. Men and women, young and old, and from different social backgrounds and levels of income would come along. They would usually be clutching paperwork of some kind – a summons from the small claims court that had arrived in the post that morning, a high court writ, final demands for rent or mortgage arrears, letters from bailiffs, possession orders and quantities of old plastic bags stuffed full of unpaid bills. I heard sad stories of people's desperation so many times – the crying, the sleepless nights, the panic attacks. Some even spoke of wanting to take their own lives. Often, the pressure of the debt had a negative impact on relationships or even brought marriages to an end.[68]

---

68 Relate, 'Money is Top Strain on Relationships', (22 March 2017). https://www.relate.org.uk/about-us/media-centre/press-releases/2017/3/13/money-top-strain-relationships; Relate, 'In Too Deep: an Investigation into Debt and Relationships', (November 2017). https://www.relate.org.uk/policy-campaigns/our-campaigns/too-deep-investigation-debt-and-relationships.

Many of these couples hadn't been unwise or even irresponsible with money. Some were suffering from the knock-on effect of redundancy or illness as it hit the family budget. Some were self-employed and struggling with cash flow, whilst others had simply found it hard to cope in a society that pushes the use of credit but offers little help in managing the resulting debt.

There have been huge concerns about the amount of unsecured debt that families have taken on, with many getting new credit cards or drawing down on existing credit arrangements simply to make interest payments.[69] Advertisements on television and pop-ups on our computer screens entice us to use credit for that 'must-have' item and to 'take the waiting out of wanting'. Payday loan companies offer short-term, high-cost credit giving the customer cash in an hour but often at colossal interest rates. They may be fine for those who can definitely pay it back, but for many it is the beginning of a descent into isolation, loneliness and sleepless nights. Plastic cards, apps, online purchases and even contactless payments make it feel as if we aren't spending *real* money and family debt increases exponentially.

Even if we are not spiralling into uncontrolled debt, the truth is that most of us will feel the pressure of financial struggles at some time in our marriages. Money worries do not discriminate on person, status or income because whatever the state of our bank balance, the temptation is always to spend that little bit more than we can afford.

I remember a time in our marriage when I overspent on the credit card and it reached the limit. I didn't tell Richard (research has found that one in seven people have hidden debt

69 Phillip Inman, 'UK credit binge approaching levels not seen since 2008 crash', *The Guardian* (4 January 2017). https://www.theguardian.com/business/2017/jan/04/uk-credit-cards-borrowing-debt-economic-crash-fears.

from a partner),[70] my sense of independence kicked in, and I mistakenly believed I could sort it out on my own. I eventually told him about it and I remember his incredible support. That incident was a timely lesson to us to: (a) not allow credit to get a head of steam, and (b) be honest and open with each other about our spending.

Most arguments aren't generally because one of us is good with money and the other bad, but because we simply have different attitudes to money and different spending priorities. Some couples have to manage tight budgets and struggle just to put food on the table, but even then we may discover that one of us may naturally be a spender, the other a saver.

Chelsea spoke about the issue of money in her marriage:

We used to row a lot about money – not so much about what we had in our bank account or the size of our overdraft limit, but about what we should be spending the money on. Sam is always thinking about the future. He wants us to save so that we can put down a deposit on a house, and sometimes talks about saving for his retirement even though that's years away! I live more in the moment. I enjoy going out for a meal or to the cinema and buying things for the kids or the flat. Understanding the difference between us has helped us manage our finances better. We don't find it easy talking about money and easily slip into blaming each other when we go overdrawn, but when we do manage to sit down and discuss it, we get back on the same wavelength, problems don't build up and it's much better for our marriage.

70 Relate, 'In Too Deep: an Investigation into Debt and Relationships' (November 2017). https://www.relate.org.uk/policy-campaigns/our-campaigns/too-deep-investigation-debt-and-relationships.

Money can be either something that causes conflict and comes between us or something we can work at together that will draw us closer and strengthen our marriage. If it *is* an issue, we can regain control by taking the following steps. They are simple to read, but perhaps more challenging to put into practice!

Dealing with Debt or Financial Worries

1. Recognize that you are not alone. Money problems can make us feel isolated, but there are many people facing the same problems.

2. Talk honestly together. One couple set up a weekly appointment – a 'money chat' meeting round the kitchen table just to check in with each other about how they were doing financially.

3. Prepare a budget. Having a family budget is a good principle to follow in all marriages, but if money is causing tension it's important to sit down together and take back control by making sure that you don't spend more than you can afford. Start by making a list of the following:

- All your income (salary, pensions, benefits)
- All your spending (everything!)
- All your outstanding debts (credit cards, loans).

This information may not be easy to work out, but its purpose is to help balance what we have coming in against what we are spending (including paying off debts). It may mean that we have to keep going back to reduce what we're spending on some items or even knocking them off the budget completely for a while.

4. If you are in debt, don't ignore it or think the problem will magically disappear. Take action. If you're not sure where to start or need more support, a debt adviser can really help you. Make sure that you go to a reputable organization for *free* advice. (See Appendix for organizations offering help and advice about budgeting and debt.)

Some debts have more serious consequences than others and the largest debt may not be the most important one to pay off first. Seek advice about priority and non-priority debts – for example, not paying the rent or mortgage may mean losing your home so is more of a priority than credit card debts.

Once all of the priority debts are paid, hit the credit/store cards. Pay at least the minimum payment on *all* credit and store cards (otherwise charges are incurred). Then choose the card that has the highest rate of interest (this appears on the statements), stop using it for further purchases and pay as much money off it each month as you possibly can. After a while, the balance will get lower and lower, and one day it will fall to zero. When you have cleared that first card, go on to attack the next most expensive card. Keep going and you will find in time that all these giants will fall.

5. Think about going back to cash for a while. Richard and I tried this several years ago as part of Care for the Family's 'Cash for a Month' challenge. It was much harder than we thought and we had many late night discussions over our respective definitions of *needs* v. *wants*! For me, that flat white when I'm out shopping is a definite *need* not a want, and Richard would say the same about that Friday evening beer after work! Even though we didn't always agree, it was a useful exercise in assessing our spending habits.

These steps are not a silver bullet, but putting them into practice can make all the difference, not just to our finances but to our marriage as well. Of course, some couples have extremely challenging financial circumstances where the issue is more about finding the money to buy food for the family than resisting a cup of coffee when we're out on the high street or going for a drink after work.

Frank had never been good with money, and when he married Leila he didn't tell her the total amount of his debt – he didn't want her to worry. But over the months and then years, his debt – and his secret – grew bigger and he felt isolated and alone. The truth of it was that they just didn't have enough cash coming in to keep their heads above water. He tried juggling the credit cards but that caught up with him as well. One day Leila suggested they book a holiday – she didn't know he had maxed out both the credit card and the overdraft, and would have no way to pay for it. He felt like a rabbit caught in the headlights and in desperation he knew he had to tell her everything. Leila felt let down and betrayed, and the trust they had between them vanished. It would be unfair to say that there were no other issues in the marriage, but this was the final straw. She packed her bags and went to live with her mum. Frank thought their marriage was over.

It was only then that a friend put him in touch with a debt counsellor. He made a long-term plan to get back control of his finances and slowly began to climb his way out of debt. It was painful, it was hard work and he had to make sacrifices – but it was worth it. 'In working to get out of debt, I got more than I bargained for,' he said. 'I got Leila back as well.'

KNOW WHERE YOU'RE GOING

Hotel lobbies, company boardrooms, doctors' waiting rooms, schools and corporation lifts are where organizations often like to display a framed list of their 'visions and values'. They are useful for companies because they encourage executives to think through not just what they do, but also who they are – the values they live by. Knowing what a company's vision and values are not only sets the direction of travel but helps keep everyday decision-making on track.

Agreed vision and values are also not a bad idea for marriages, as they highlight the things that we believe are important in life and give us a picture of how we want to spend our time together. They make it very clear what the non-negotiables are and help us make big decisions as well as guiding us on some of the little ones. In other words, we have a framework for what to say 'yes' to and what to say 'no' to.

A friend recently bought us a black and white picture, which now takes pride of place in our kitchen. It reads: 'Have hope. Be strong. Play hard. Live in the moment. Smile often. Dream big. Remember you are loved. And never, never give up.' If we had designed it ourselves we would no doubt have added some more, but these values are not a bad place to start in giving some bearings for our life together – compass readings that we return

'It's been a few years now. Do you think it's time we started to implement our family vision?'

to when challenges come our way.

Marriage preparation courses often encourage couples to list the things or people that take their time and attention (family, friends, work, voluntary work, children, parents, pets, each other) and then list them in order of priority. In fact, it's not a bad list to make no matter how long we've been married. Agreeing these priorities together will help us make decisions about what to do when life seems too busy and everyone is clamouring for our attention. Whilst there are some obvious priorities (our spouse should be number one and definitely above the pug!), the point of the list is that we work out what is important for *us*. We can then create a unique set of values that give meaning and purpose to our marriage.

Research shows that couples do best when they have a shared vision for their marriage, which develops over time.[71] As our marriage progresses we become more secure together; we don't have to keep working on the foundations and fine details of our relationship – that part comes more naturally – and so we have the capacity to take a step back and look at where we are going.

As well as agreeing the people or things that have first demand on our time, we can also look at the bigger picture – our vision for our marriage and our goals for the season we are currently in. This isn't as grand or daunting as it might sound. It certainly isn't about creating a five-year strategic plan to display on the kitchen notice board. More likely, it might simply mean sitting down over a glass of wine or a cup of coffee, looking at our current circumstances, skills, gifts, time and opportunities, and thinking through how best to use them.

Sometimes, it will be as much as we can do to get through everyday life – and that needs to be our focus, but there may also

71 R. Gutteridge, *Enduring Relationships: The Evolution of Long-Lasting Marriage,* unpublished PhD thesis.

be times when we can help each other fulfil a long-held dream or when we have the capacity and resource to give to others. We may love being hospitable and using our home to invite others round for fun and laughter or as a refuge from the storms of life. We may have young children and so our attention will be on our home life and school activities. We may want to travel or set up a small business together. We may have a heart for the poor or disadvantaged and volunteer together to help charities, our local church or faith community. This is not about finding extra things to do on top of a busy week, but about discovering how to use our marriage to help others in line with our passions, gifts and opportunities.

When we take time today to think through the vision and values for our marriage, we set priorities that will affect it in five, ten, twenty and thirty years from now. We are orientating ourselves around a 'shared future' together.

… We know where we are going.

PREPARE FOR THE
HEADWINDS

I remember having a go at sea-kayaking when we were on holiday. Wales isn't exactly known for its Mediterranean climate and we had to battle against the elements; there was a particularly strong headwind which made paddling hard work, and it was a real challenge to get back to shore.

But headwinds don't just occur in the middle of a stormy sea; they happen in a marriage too. Life is challenging and we all have our share of disappointments and crises. Some are expected and some come out of the blue; some have only a brief impact and others change our lives forever. They could be financial pressures, illness, disability, bereavement, infertility, issues with children, work pressures, unemployment, family conflict, tragedies in our local community or any number of other situations. And the nature of marriage means that what affects one of us affects both of us. Research bears this out: 'When a crisis hits, a husband or wife is not just a kindly bystander or good friend. He or she is a direct player in the unfolding drama ...'[72]

Another important factor in times of crisis is how we react. The following quote is attributed to Winston Churchill: 'Kites

72 Judith S. Wallerstein and Sandra Blakeslee, *The Good Marriage: How and Why Love Lasts*, p.121.

'We may have to make a few adjustments in our life for a while ...'

rise highest against the wind – not with it.' I have recently spoken to two couples who have faced incredible struggles in their marriages. Whilst your challenges may be different, I believe there are seeds in their stories that can sow hope in any marriage going through a tough time.

Rachel and Ian met when she was an eighteen-year-old school-leaver. Ian was five years older and had just returned from college. They started to date, their friendship developed, and a year and a half later they married. Rachel tells their story:

Like most couples, we began married life in a warm romantic glow of love, believing nothing would ever change. Now, almost thirty-seven years later, we are still together and still in love, but there have been challenges in those years that could have destroyed it all.

After eighteen happy years, we were confronted by a tsunami that changed everything. Ian suffered an episode of severe depression that altered the equilibrium of our marriage. In time, he recovered and life returned to normal, until nine years later when the depression returned with increasing severity. He has just had a third bout of illness. Each depression saw him hospitalized for two months, with the impact of his illness becoming worse with each episode.

It's hard to paint a picture of what it's like to watch the man you love disappear before your eyes into a cloud of darkness. He was still present physically, but absent in every other way, and in the acute phase of his illness, I became his carer. Everything in our relationship was different. It was a bleak and isolating journey. No aspect of our marriage escaped the effects of his depression as he battled through his treatment.

Thankfully, he is making a recovery and whilst we never wanted this experience, we have learnt some valuable lessons, born out of pain, which I am grateful for.

Reflecting on the journey, Rachel identified some things that helped their marriage survive:

I had promised to love Ian 'in sickness and in health', so each morning, no matter how hard it was, I set out to try and keep that promise. It was easier to do when I paused and remembered the qualities I loved in him and the fun, laughter and good times we'd had. And it was easier to do when I remembered that his illness was not his fault. We learnt to celebrate and find joy in the day-to-day ordinary things of life. Rather than being in denial, it helped to accept that although this illness may limit our plans, we still had a future.

Perhaps the most important lesson I have learnt is that marriages are not perfect, nor the people in them. But although we cannot make them perfect, we can be purposeful about investing in each other, supporting each other and trying to create a partnership in which we are companions for the journey of life.

The second couple, Sheridan and Merryn, faced a very different but equally devastating challenge. I had the privilege of interviewing Sheridan when recording Care for the Family's

DVD resource, *The Marriage Sessions*, and he told me their story:

Merryn and I met at college, married shortly after, and five years later decided to start a family. Although we didn't know it at the time, that decision ushered in a series of disappointments and challenges that threatened to shake our marriage to the core. After the excitement and anticipation of making that decision to have a baby, month after month we found ourselves on a rollercoaster of high expectation followed by crashing disappointment. We spent the next ten years trying to conceive. We tried everything – special diets, supplements, IVF – and two years later went on the adoption register. Every day we waited for the phone to ring, but the call never came. After our final round of IVF we had the incredible news that Merryn was pregnant, only to be told a few weeks later on Christmas Eve that she wasn't. With that cruel twist, our decade-long dream of having a child was at an end.

I asked Sheridan how this had affected them as a couple:

There were so many issues to work though. Should we continue with IVF? Should we adopt? We weren't on the same page and there was real tension between us that seemed impossible to overcome. So often, everything in me wanted to leave the room and not stay to work through things together. A breakthrough moment came one afternoon when we met with an IVF counsellor. She explained that the IVF process can put a tremendous strain on couples, not just physically and emotionally but on their relationship. At that moment, Merryn spoke up: 'Sheridan and I have agreed that our marriage is more important than having a child.' The counsellor seemed surprised and let her professional guard slip for a moment. 'I'm so glad you said that,' she said. 'Just yesterday, I had a very different conversation with a couple sitting where you are now. The wife said to her husband: 'If IVF doesn't work this time, I'm afraid our relationship is over.'

Looking back, the decision to put our marriage first – to put it above the pain, the disappointments and the broken dreams – is what got us through. It's been a long story, but we eventually decided this meant leaving Australia and moving to the UK. Merryn was offered a job in Oxford and we have started our lives again.

We married in order to do life together and that included sharing in the fulfilment of each other's dreams. Facing the disappointment of those broken dreams and choosing to start again with new ones has strengthened our relationship and made us resilient. There is one greater tragedy than a broken dream and that is to have your marriage forever defined by it.[73]

Country music singer Jimmy Dean said in an interview, 'I can't change the direction of the wind, but I can adjust my sails to always reach my destination.'[74] Both the couples I have just mentioned have done just that. They have faced incredible

73 Based on an interview with Care for the Family featured on *The Marriage Sessions* DVD course. Read more about Sheridan and Merryn's story in Sheridan's book, *Resurrection Year*.
74 Jimmy Dean, 'Interview', *Iowa City Press-Citizen* (21 January 1987), p.1c.

headwinds in their marriages that could easily have knocked them off course, but their determination not to apportion blame, to face the challenges and to work through them together, has enabled them to keep going. Looking at them today, I see a strength and resilience that I know they wouldn't previously have thought possible. They chose to battle the headwinds and, although they may have a different future to the one they originally planned, it is a future they are facing *together*.

'Happy anniversary. I got us some medals to
celebrate getting this far ...'

WHEN THE MUSIC CHANGES, SO DOES THE DANCE

The following remark is ascribed to Albert Einstein (although whether his genius actually extended from physics to psychology I am not so sure!): 'Men marry women with the hope they will never change. Women marry men with the hope they *will* change. Invariably they are both disappointed.' The truth is that marriage is dynamic. In fact, in the course of our married life we may find that we are married to two or more people – our partner is different to the person they used to be. We all change (for both better and worse!) and our circumstances change as well. Our marriages are a work in progress as we navigate the different seasons of life, and they do best when we pay attention to those changes. Whilst some of these will be unexpected, many are predictable and simply represent the different stages of life, but each stage brings its own set of challenges and opportunities.

Previous chapters have already looked at the first season of marriage, when husband and wife set out on the adventure of forging a new identity together. It's a time for discoveries – some a delight, others less so! If children come along, the next season involves readjusting identity and roles as we move from just being partners to being parents as well. And if the years with primary children are exhausting physically (and they are!), having teenagers in the home can be equally exhausting emotionally. Both can take their toll on our marriage.

Before we know it, midlife is upon us and children are leaving home. This (in theory!) is the season that Richard and I are in now. Until now, our role as parents has been the main strand of the bond between us, and we are discovering it takes some readjustment as we discover a new focus for our marriage. For the best part of the last fifteen years, our weekends had a familiar routine – providing a taxi service for our children (and their many friends) on a Friday night and standing on the side of a netball court or rugby, football or hockey pitch for most of Saturday. When our youngest left for university we didn't know what to do with ourselves on a Saturday. It was an unexpected surprise!

One of the reasons it's important to invest in our marriage in the early years is to ensure that we don't lose each other in the all-consuming season of parenting. Years later, when we are facing each other across the kitchen table without the cushion of our teenagers' energy and banter, we still need to have something to talk about. One father, who had been looking forward to the empty nest as an opportunity for him and his wife to have fun and discover new interests together, said: 'It's been a big adjustment. Our kids were noisy and messy and I couldn't wait for them to go, but now the house is quiet … and much too tidy!'

Spending more time together at this time and rediscovering our friendship can bring us closer together and fill the gap caused by children finding pastures new. If we don't maintain our relationship while they are still at home with us then it may be that, on the very first evening after they have gone, we look at our husband or wife and wonder who they are.

The empty nest paves the way for retirement, and in that season of life especially, the quality or otherwise of our marriage can have a significant effect on our health.[75] As people are living longer, many couples can expect to have a good number of years post-retirement. Researchers have known for about a decade that divorce can depress the immune system's function. Now they have found that not only do happily married people avoid this drop in immune function, it may even be getting an extra boost. Marriage expert John Gottman commented: 'I often think that if fitness buffs spent just ten percent of their weekly workout time – say, twenty minutes a day – working on their marriage instead of their bodies, they would get three times the health benefits they derive from climbing the StairMaster!'[76]

I remember talking recently to Helen who retired with her husband, Jim, ten years ago. I have always admired their marriage and especially the way they used the opportunity of retirement to take up new activities. They bought a camper van, headed off round the country and got involved in their community. She gave me some wise advice: 'We love retirement and it gave us the opportunity to try lots of new things. We aren't as fit now and are so glad we took that opportunity when we could. Don't leave it too late.'

Many couples worry that when they retire all that extra enforced togetherness will be like opening a Pandora's box of irritations and frustrations. Boredom and isolation can also be a hazard. It is not always possible, and it's certainly not a magic

75 C. M. Proulx and L. A. Snyder-Rivas, 'The longitudinal associations between marital happiness, problems, and self-rated health', *Journal of Family Psychology* (2013), *27*(2), p.194–202.
76 John Gottman, *The Seven Principles for Making Marriage Work* (Orion, 2007), p.6.

formula, but investing in friends and outside interests helps protect the inner world of marriage.

In some marriages the challenge of ill health or an age gap can put an extra strain on the relationship as one of the couple becomes the caregiver. I have seen this in my own parents' marriage when my eighty-year-old mother became the primary caregiver for my father, who was seventeen years older than her. He was the kindest, gentlest, most generous and undemanding man, and yet caring for him took patience, courage and sacrifice on my mother's part.

I love this description by Judith Wallerstein of the changing seasons in her marriage:

I am aware of the physical changes of aging in my body: my right knee is getting stiff with arthritis, and I walk more slowly than before. When my husband and I walk together, as we do daily, I notice that he has slowed his pace because of my infirmity … It goes without saying that he will accommodate to my need and we will both walk more slowly …

When we return home, he usually has some tasks he urgently wants to attend to, and that is fine with me; I know that if he doesn't do them he will be unhappy …

Marriage is made up of the little things, both the good and the bad. The little changes, too, add to the important rhythms of life. The changing interactions between my husband and me are part of this major chapter in my married life. We are building a marriage now just as surely as when we were younger, as surely as when we returned from our honeymoon and started out on our life together. The thousand and one changes in our relationship, in observing each other and adjusting to each other, are no different today. Except that we are better at it – we have had a lot of practice.[77]

A lovely African proverb says: 'When the music changes, so does the dance.' Whether it's the season to dance a jive, a polka or a waltz in our marriage, it's a good reminder to keep in step together.

77 Judith S. Wallerstein and Sandra Blakeslee, *The Good Marriage: How and Why Love Lasts*, p.327–328.

LOVE IS A CHOICE

We have four children and just like the proverbial buses, there was no sign of impending nuptials from them for twenty-six years (perhaps understandably for the first sixteen!), then three weddings came along within a year. So in that twelve-month period, not only did our bank balance take a hit, but I became an expert on 'wedmin' and Pinterest, and a world authority on where to buy a hat.

The three weddings were wonderful days, and I have so many happy memories, but one of the most moving moments in each service was when our children made their marriage vows, promising to be there for each other in the ups and downs of marriage, whatever the future held.

'I will love you for better …,' and the vow prompts, 'but don't forget worse.' 'I will love you if we are rich …,' and the vow says, 'and what if you are poor?' 'I will love you if you are well …,' and the vow adds, 'consider sickness too.' Like any parent, I hope that those vows won't be called upon for our children, but in my heart I know there will come a time when they will. Pressure comes to every marriage.

Rob Parsons wrote about a couple he had counselled. They were in their mid-twenties, had a baby girl aged six months, and were about to divorce. Rob asked the man why he was leaving his young family. He replied: 'I don't feel in love any more.' Rob described what happened next:

As [the man] spoke, I couldn't help but gaze at the little bundle that his wife cradled in her arms. I said, 'Did nobody tell you when you married that there will be times when the feeling of love will diminish? Did nobody warn you that love that lasts, does so by loving – at least for a time – with not the heart, but the will? Did nobody say that unless you understand this, you are doomed to move from relationship to relationship at the mercy of your feelings?' He looked genuinely surprised. 'No,' he said. 'Nobody told me that.'

I gazed at his daughter asleep in her mother's arms. The first man in her life was about to walk out on her … and 'nobody told him that'.[78]

Despite the culture change in our attitude towards recycling and, more recently, to plastics, we are still a consumer society. Built-in obsolescence means that our mobile phone breaks and we take it to be repaired, but come away with an upgrade instead. We use disposable nappies (phew!) but also disposable cups, disposable bags and disposable razors. This way of thinking is engrained in our culture and has crept into how we treat our relationships and our marriages.

Maybe we don't find each other as attractive as we did when we first fell in love. (As someone once said, 'When we get older, the broad mind and the narrow waist have a habit of changing places!') Maybe we are struggling with illness or financial pressure. Maybe we feel bored, irritable or simply feel that the sparkle seems to have gone out of our relationship. We just don't *feel* in love. The question that comes into every marriage at these times is this: do we work at it, or do we exchange it for a different model?

78 Rob Parsons, *The Sixty Minute Family: An Hour To Transform Your Relationships Forever* (Lion Hudson, 2010), p.89.

At our marriage events, we talk about 'January love'. It's easy to love in the warm days of summer when the sun shines out of a cloudless sky. But what about when the sky is grey and the storm clouds gather? What does it take to love in January? Is it possible for a marriage that seems dead to fight through the hard frost and find love again? No marriage can survive on iron will alone, but sometimes, at least for a while, loving our husband or wife may need to be an act of the will – a choice.

In my work at Care for the Family, I've seen more than enough painful situations to know that it's not possible to keep *every* marriage alive. But I have also seen many couples who have come back from the brink of divorce because – against all the odds – they have chosen to fight to keep their love alive and, in that process, they have rediscovered a relationship they wouldn't have thought possible.

A beautiful paragraph from Louis de Bernières' novel *Captain Corelli's Mandolin* is often read at weddings. Dr Iannis is giving some fatherly advice to his daughter, Pelagia, when he realizes that she has fallen in love with Captain Corelli. He says:

When you fall in love, it is a temporary madness. It erupts like an earthquake, and then it subsides. And when it subsides, you have to make a decision. You have to work out whether your roots have so entwined together that it is inconceivable that you should ever part. Because this is what love is. Love is not breathlessness, it is not excitement … It is not lying awake at night imagining he is kissing every cranny of your body … That is just being 'in love', which any fool can do. Love itself is what is left over when being in love has burned away … Your mother and I had it, we had roots that grew towards each other underground, and when all the pretty blossom had fallen from our branches we found that we were one tree and not two.[79]

That little phrase 'one tree and not two' reminds me of a special sight it is my privilege to witness once a year in the playground of my children's old school. Many years ago – I imagine even before the school was built – two cherry trees were planted side by side, one white and one pink. Over the years and through the seasons the two sets of roots have entwined and have grown into one trunk – they have become one. Every May when the tree is in blossom, half the flowers are white and half are pink. My hope and prayer for my marriage, and for yours, is that as we choose love, our roots will entwine together over the years so that in a beautiful way, two will become one.

But, of course, marriage works best when it is not about 'us', and in the same way as the cherry tree is there for everyone to enjoy, our marriages can have an influence beyond our own happiness and enjoyment. They can be a power for good not just in the lives of our families, friends and communities but in society as a whole, passing on love, security and values to generations to come.

As this book comes to a close, I want to tell you about a remarkable conversation I had recently with a London taxi driver. I think that what he shared with me that day as we crawled through the traffic along Park Lane sums up so perfectly what is at the heart of marriage. He had been happily married for thirty-five years. They had gone through the usual ups and downs that most couples experience, but a couple of years ago his wife got out of bed to go to the bathroom and she stumbled. A few weeks later she reached for a can in the supermarket and it slipped from her hand. She underwent a battery of tests,

79 Louis de Bernières, *Captain Corelli's Mandolin* (Vintage, 1998) p.344–45.

and eventually they received the news that she had an illness that was affecting her muscles. The doctor advised her that she might be able to delay its progression if she did some weight-bearing exercise. She tried to cycle, but her balance wasn't good enough; she joined a gym, but she wasn't strong enough to use the equipment. Then a flier came through their letterbox advertising ballroom dancing classes, so they decided to give them a go. He said to me: 'Her balance wasn't good, and it certainly wasn't *Strictly*, but we managed to get through most of the dances together.'

A short time afterwards, they were having a cup of tea together and he said to her, 'You tried cycling, you tried the gym and that special machine – what's so different about the dancing?' She was quiet for a moment, then she looked at him and smiled. 'You honestly don't know? … It's because you're holding me.'

I have worked in the family arena one way or another for thirty years. I know that often there are no easy answers, and I also know it's a million times easier to write about this stuff than it is to live it day by day. Nevertheless, throughout those years I have come across real couples in real – and often challenging situations – who have inspired me to believe that it is worth investing in our marriages. I wrote this book to be part of that investment. But if I could leave you with just one line from it that sums up the heart of a good marriage, it would be the one spoken by a woman who discovered the truth of the old proverb: 'Two are better than one … one can help the other up'.

And that line is simply this: '*It's because you're holding me.*'

If you forget everything else about marriage, remember this.

APPENDIX

Further Information and Support

The following organizations offer helpful advice and support on some of the issues covered in this book. As specific web addresses change from time to time, it may be necessary occasionally to search for the relevant information on an organization's home page or a general web browser.

Marriage

CARE FOR THE FAMILY
www.careforthefamily.org.uk
Care for the Family aims to promote strong family life and help those who face family difficulties. It provides marriage and relationship, parenting, and bereavement support through events, resources, courses, training and volunteer networks.
Tel. 029 2081 0800

MARRIAGE CARE
www.marriagecare.org.uk
Marriage Care provides relationship support services including couples counselling, relationship and marriage preparation.
Tel. 0800 389 3801

RELATE
www.relate.org.uk
Relate offers counselling services and advice on marriage and parenting.
Tel: 0300 003 0396

THE COUPLE CONNECTION
https://thecoupleconnection.net
A relationship support service run by One Plus One which provides a wide range of articles, self-assessment tools, activities, quizzes, exercises and courses to help people to strengthen their relationships.
Tel: 020 3096 7871 (One Plus One)

THE MARRIAGE COURSE
http://themarriagecourses.org
The Marriage Course is for couples who are seeking to strengthen their relationship. It is based on Christian principles but is designed for all couples with or without a church background.
Tel: 0845 644 7533

Money and Debt

THE MONEY ADVICE SERVICE
The Beginner's Guide to Managing your Money
www.moneyadviceservice.org.uk/en/articles/beginners-guide-to-managing-your-money

THE MONEY SAVING EXPERT
The Budget Planner
www.moneysavingexpert.com/banking/Budget-planning#free

CITIZENS ADVICE
www.citizensadvice.org.uk
Citizens Advice offers free, independent, confidential and impartial debt advice through its web chat service.
Tel: 03444 111 444 (England); 028 9023 1120 (Northern Ireland); 0808 800 9060 (Scotland); 03444 77 20 20 (Wales)

CHRISTIANS AGAINST POVERTY
www.capuk.org
Christians Against Poverty (CAP) is a national debt counselling charity offering hope and a solution to anyone in debt through its unique, in-depth service.
Tel: 01274 760720

DEBT ADVICE FOUNDATION
www.debtadvicefoundation.org
Debt Advice Foundation is a national debt advice and education charity offering free, confidential support and advice to anyone worried about debt.
Tel: 0800 043 40 50

NATIONAL DEBTLINE
www.mymoneysteps.org
National Debtline offers free debt advice by phone and online through its My Money Steps tool and its web guides, fact sheets and sample letters.
Tel: 0808 808 4000

PAYPLAN
www.payplan.com
PayPlan's services include free, confidential online chat with
debt help experts, a debt help request form, and a wealth of
online resources.
Tel: 0800 280 2816

Pornography

THE NAKED TRUTH PROJECT
www.thenakedtruthproject.com
A charity with a Christian ethos that tackles the damaging
effects of pornography by providing resources, workshops and
recovery programmes accessible to those of any or no faith.

RELATE
www.relate.org.uk
Relate offers counselling services for every type of relationship
nationwide. It can help with breaking free from pornography.
Tel: 0300 003 0396

SEX AND PORN ADDICTION HELP
www.sexaddictionhelp.co.uk
A free self-help recovery resource for people struggling with sex
or pornography addiction.

Care for the Family is a national charity which aims to promote strong family life and help those who face family difficulties. Working throughout the UK and the Isle of Man, we provide parenting, relationship and bereavement support through our events, courses, training and other resources. For more information, and to explore our wide range of resources on all aspects of family life, visit our website at **www.careforthefamily.org.uk.**

Muddy
Pearl